ELEVATE YOUR LEADERSHIP

ROBERT PIZZINI

Those who have experienced a military professional life know that leadership is a critical skill set, not just for officers but for every participant in a military endeavor. Leaders are prepared, trained, coached, and mentored aggressively because military history teaches us that leadership is often, the swing factor that paves the way to success. Robert Pizzini's Elevate Your Leadership begins with this same military premise as it guides readers toward and clear understanding of what leadership is, and what it is not. The book is logical, and insightful. It provides the reader with a progressive learning experience that will prove invaluable for existing leaders or those who aspire to lead organizations. Filled with practical lessons, tips, tools, and leadership philosophy, Elevate Your Leadership deserves a prominent place on everybody's bookshelf!

Marty Strong

CEO, Author, Retired SEAL Officer

Robert Pizzini is truly an American hero that has paved the road for others to follow. His book, 'Elevate Your Leadership' has shown me how to craft my own leadership brand while building the confidence needed to scale my own company. The lessons learned in this book has been instilled in my companies corporate structure and has helped us grow when other competitors around me been left behind. I highly recommended, 'Elevate Your Leadership' to both executives and business leaders looking to maximize their space in the world of business today.

Michael Alexander Beas

Founder Atlas Elite Publishing Partners

'There's no one more qualified to define 'leadership' than Bob Pizzini. His 26-year career as an Explosive Ordnance Disposal (EOD) Technician in the US Navy prepared him for all kinds of high-wire situations that can only be acquired through experience. If that's not a leader, I don't know what is. This book based on true, tested skills can be applied to private sector businesses immediately. Pick up a copy of Bob's book and elevate your leadership to new heights!'

Jeffrey Hayzlett

Primetime TV & Podcast Host, Speaker, Author and Part-Time Cowboy

Elements of leadership include risk, trust, teamwork, a clearly defined and desired outcome, and confidence in the pursuit of an objective. All these elements are represented in the cover photo of the author exiting a helicopter in Virginia Beach, Virginia.

Cover Design by Michael Beas

Copyright Robert Pizzini © 2022

All rights reserved. No part of this book may be used or reproduced by any means, graphic, electronic, or mechanical, including photocopying, recording, taping or by any information storage retrieval system without the written permission of the author except in the case of brief quotations embodied in critical articles and reviews.

ISBN: 979-8-9869353-4-8

C-SUITEPUBLISHING

DEDICATION

This book is dedicated first and foremost to my wife Julie, and our two teenage children. Lessons in leadership apply at home as well as in the workplace. Discussions at the dinner table, poolside, and while driving to and from hockey and volleyball with my family helped develop key concepts in this volume.

I am also greatly appreciative of my active-duty leaders, teammates, and mentors. I miss working alongside the men and women who wear the cloth of our nation and execute the missions that keep us safe. Actually, what I really miss is working with a team of professionals to execute some of the coolest stuff on the planet. My career in US Navy Special Operations, my leaders, and my teammates, prepared me for entrepreneurship in the private sector. Among the many who have helped me along the way, my EOD teammate Mark Sanders has mentored me while on active duty and continues to provide guidance and support eleven years after we both retired. I am grateful, and I hope this book will help others transition from active duty to the private sector with great success.

Next, I dedicate the first attempt at writing a complete volume to my great team at iFLY Virginia Beach. Among the seven people on the leadership team, five of us, Jason, Misty, Ray, Kendall, my wife Julie, and I have been working together since 2014, when construction began. Amy and Tyler have been onboard for five years or so, and the trust and synergy that developed over the past eight years is remarkable to say the least. In the military, our team lifecycle is usually two to three years, from pre-deployment training to deployment and post-deployment. It is a great pleasure to work with the same people for so many years.

ACKNOWLEDGEMENTS

A perfect example of a successful SEAL transitioning to effective corporate leader is Marty Strong, whose two books (*Be Nimble* and *Be Visionary*) outline the tactics he used to transition from leading SEAL teams to leading multimillion-dollar businesses as a successful CEO. His experiences and mentorship throughout the process of writing this book have been invaluable as I documented my own lessons learned.

Next, I would like to acknowledge the many contributions made by my circle of friends and professionals who are too numerous to name individually. Fellow hockey coach John read early chapters and offered many notes and suggestions for clarifications. Allison Krug, a fellow hockey parent and technical writer, jumped at the chance to coach me through this writing process and has been instrumental in helping me deliver a concise and meaningful message.

Finally, I would like to express gratitude to my fellow executives in the C-Suite Network who served as steady mentors throughout the writing journey, podcast launch and book publication. I'm grateful to each person who has touched my life, and by doing so, contributed directly to the many lessons illuminated in this book.

CONTENTS

Dedication 4
Acknowledgements 5
Preface 9
Forward 13
Ground Rules 16
Introduction 19
Part I: The Art of Leadership 26
Chapter 1: The Challenge of Modern Leadership 27
Chapter 2: Defining Moments 44
Chapter 3: Constructing Your Leadership foundation ... 58
Personal Leadership Profile 73
Chapter 4: Eleven Critical Traits 75
Chapter 5: Read and React 90
Chapter 6: Diversity Equity and Inclusion 106
Part II: The Science of Leadership 126
  Wellness Worksheet 129
Chapter 7: Sleep 130
Chapter 8: Hydration 136
Chapter 9: Nutrition 141
Chapter 10: Exercise 147

Chapter 11: Brain-Heart Link 153
Chapter 12: Lifelong learning 160
Go 166
Note to Readers 168
About the Author 169

LEADERSHIP IS A PERISHABLE SKILL...USE IT OR LOSE IT.

PREFACE

Are you ready to get out of your comfort zone? Are you bold enough to take the next step in evolving and expanding your ability to lead yourself and others? Are you ready to awaken to key aspects of leadership? This book will evolve and expand your confidence and competence if you are bold enough to take the first step, which you have already—simply by acquiring the book and reading my personal appeal. You will awaken to key aspects of leadership upon reading each page in this volume, and you will realize the value of these aspects more and more each day, each month, and each year, throughout your professional life.

> In Part I, The Art of Leadership, you will assemble the elements of your personal leadership styles and power types, then we move to Part II, The Science of Leadership, which delves into the physical health and mental wellness of a good leader. Throughout, you will gain practical steps to improve your daily performance as a leader.

Leadership is a perishable skill. Use it or lose it. Musicians rehearse, athletes train, and scholars research. Leading others is no different. Successful organizations have strong leaders who are dedicated to lifelong learning. As General Mattis stated in his book *Call Sign Chaos*, "be brilliant at the basics." The basics of leadership begin with a solid foundation, built on the principles outlined in Part I, The Art of Leadership. Your foundation will endure throughout your lifetime through abiding by the principles in Part II, The Science of Leadership. However, this book is not an academic guide. It focuses on specific actions you can take to develop your confidence and competence, which will greatly expand your comfort zone.

Boots-on-the-ground experience

The guidance presented in this book has been learned, lived, and implemented over my 26-year U.S. Navy Special Operations career, where the penalty for mishandling explosives is usually of high consequence. After my transition to the private sector just over a decade ago, I realized the significance of having a fully developed leadership foundation. This foundation, like that of a skyscraper, is both deep and wide, yet is largely unseen by others. I want to share what I have learned to help you develop, sustain, and advance your leadership brand, and develop leaders amongst your team. Leadership development is not just a military principle. The habits we formed in Special Operations helped me to build, lead and deploy teams that successfully completed missions around the world.

After serving in uniform, I transitioned to the private sector and launched a very visible and unique multimillion-dollar venture. Failure was not an option then, or now. As we say in Navy Explosive Ordnance Disposal (EOD) "initial success, or total failure." After ten years of growing my business and investing in my community through the Chamber of Commerce, public school system, youth sports, and other endeavors, it became clear that many of the leadership skills I formed in the military were serving my team and my community well. These skills are by now a habit, and I rely on them daily in all facets of my life. What if you and those rising through the ranks in your organization could also develop proven leadership habits?

The concepts and methods presented here are drawn on personal experience, formal education, and many training events throughout my professional life. I firmly believe that the triad of experience, education, and training is required to develop solid leadership. I credit my efforts to build a solid foundation in leadership for providing clarity when the fog was thick, such as when COVID-19 caused all businesses in Virginia to close to the public on March 23, 2020. This was a time when I had to dig deep, and I had to make bold decisions which were sometimes not very popular, especially with my banker. However, as of this writing, my business is thriving once again as my team, led by a first-class General Manager and five additional management level leaders, demonstrated resiliency throughout this pandemic.

In addition to my own personal experience, I also drew on the insights of leadership experts. This book is informed by conversations with experts in leadership, C-level executives, academics, military strategists, psychologists, hockey coaches, small business owners, community leaders, and people in a wide range of industries. These conversations have been distilled in a variety of media—podcasts, book chapters, videos, and references within the text. If you want to explore any of these concepts further, the resources are there. In my experience, people arrive at clarity through conversation and experimentation, so take the opportunity to delve into the topics presented here further with your team and build your capacity for leadership at the same time. I often share items that I read or encounter with my team to get their take. Introducing new topics for conversation is a great leadership method to keep your team sharp. On several occasions I bought a book I had just finished reading for all 40 people on my team. For example, all newly hired teammates receive a book entitled *The High Performance Workplace*, authored by two colleagues of mine, Sue Bingham and Bob Dusin.

Who is this book for?

Whether you are a seasoned executive in the C-Suite, or you are an emerging leader wondering if this book is for you—it is. For the executives, this practical guide will reinforce and validate what you *should* already know, while presenting opportunities for growth that you may or may not have considered. It is current, relevant, and responds to the challenges of today's leadership environment.

The emerging leader will appreciate the specific guidance provided – I will coach you through the process of building habits which create competence and confidence. This book is born of an authentic desire to help you become the leader you have always aspired to be.

During my career in the military and now as a successful entrepreneur, I have gotten to know and appreciate people with a wide range of leadership qualities. Some have been stereotypical leaders—confident, bold, and assertive extroverts. However, some of the most effective leaders, in my experience, do not have all these traits. Often, these emerging leaders did not always appreciate how to weave their innate strengths, experiences, and abilities into a cohesive package. They needed a coach or a book like this to help them build confidence.

You may be feeling the fog of leadership, and your energy may be low.

Mine was, too, roughly seven years after I retired from the military. That is when I began researching how to recover my former vigor and vision. By 2019, I had not only recovered but improved my capacity to lead and I wanted to share my newfound energy and clarity with others. I launched an executive leadership coaching seminar "Elevate Your Leadership" and through these leadership events I had the opportunity to hear firsthand from entrepreneurs, corporate and community leaders, and industry professionals, the need for specific development in leadership so they can build and lead their teams. Throughout my professional life, I researched widely while living in the US and abroad, fighting in a war, teaching at the university level, interviewing other professionals, and operating a business with 40 employees, all with the intent of delivering a life-changing leadership experience to elevate those who dare to strive for perfection while knowing it will never be. This book incorporates these insights to help you evolve your natural leadership abilities.

In other words, this book was not written first, *then* tested—it is built on real-world interactions and experiences, which I weave into every chapter.

Are you ready to invest in yourself?

As we proceed, I will discuss the art and the science of leadership. Although the concept that leadership is both an art and a science is not new, the way that I define and apply the elements of leadership will be new to you. They are presented in an intuitive and practical way so that you can readily integrate them into your life. Through this framework you will discover a fresh and energizing way to approach your leadership. Yes, this book will literally energize you. In fact, part II is intended to do just that…give you greater energy that infuses not only the rest of your day but the rest of your professional life.

Each chapter begins with the bottom-line up front (**BLUF**) so you know your mission, and my intent. We close with a practical **DRILL** that enables you to practice…to rehearse, and to execute.

I hope that you find this to be an enjoyable way to get out of your comfort zone—both personally and professionally—because you will notice immediate benefits on Day 1. Guaranteed.

Thank you for joining me in this journey.

FORWARD

The world of special operations is complicated, challenging, and everchanging. Robert Pizzini survived this crucible of elite performance, transitioning from technical enlisted expert to seasoned warrior and commissioned naval leader. For twenty-six years, Robert earned peer approval as a respected Explosive Ordnance Disposal operator and then evolved into an exceptional special operations leader and planner. Bomb disposal experts have performed a unique role in all of America's modern wars but the two decade long Global War on Terror was especially challenging. Robert found himself, again and again, on the leading edge of our counterterrorism effort. There is no doubt his courage and keen acumen resulted in many lives saved, both our service men and women, and those of civilians who are so often the casual collateral damage when terrorists strike.

What lessons can be gleaned from such a dramatic and terrifying career? The answer is plenty! Robert is a lifelong learning machine. As his time in uniform came to a close, he looked out at the horizon and realized he had a distinct set of skills better executed on a battlefield, not in a boardroom. His initial self-inventory was revealing and sobering. While the Navy had provided him with millions of dollars of sophisticated training, very little related to the commercial world. Over time his reflections revealed it was the soft skills and deep experience he'd gained as a special operations leader that were clearly applicable in the private sector. These included psychological resiliency, confidence, poise under stress, planning knowledge, and an ability to communicate and inspire. Robert also realized he was a risk taker who knew how to assess and appreciate an opportunity when he saw one. It was time to apply these significant strengths in his new life.

An interesting thing happened as Robert segued from leading special operators to becoming an entrepreneur and businessman. He realized real leadership wasn't taught in business schools, and it wasn't taught in companies. In fact, he discovered in most organizations leadership wasn't even defined correctly. People were conflating management with leadership. How could this be the case? After more than two decades in uniform, experiencing the results of both bad and good leadership, he knew in his heart leadership was one of the most crucial components of success. Yet, he wasn't finding it in the commercial environment. This dilemma was at first puzzling and disturbing, but after a while he began to see his purpose. He was a leader. He knew what leadership was and how to grow, build, and develop leaders. Besides leading in his personal life and in his early business endeavors, he knew in his gut that he had a higher calling. To show others the way.

Leadership is a complex set of interdisciplinary skills rooted in a keen sense of human nature and behavior. Leaders can be born to the craft. They may display leadership traits when they are young and in time are asked by others to lead. Leading frequently allows people to become better leaders. Eventually these "natural" leaders enter the adult world ready to do more. However, leadership can also be taught. This is something Robert understood as he rose through the Navy's ranks. He observed leadership training and watched closely as newly trained leaders accepted responsibility and forged ahead, destined to both fail and succeed as they grew and evolved over time. He was a product of this same process: making mistakes, learning about his strengths and his weaknesses; watching his peers and superiors struggle as leaders. It was a teachable capability, and he was determined to refine his leadership skills, to become a great leader.

Within a few years of leaving the service, Robert was already writing down his theories and ideas about leadership in the private sector. He was sought out by other business professionals, owners, and experts for his insights and leadership knowledge. He became an investor in a business enterprise and immediately applied his prior leadership skills to the task. He also began to codify and sharpen his opinions and insights into a curriculum of leadership development. First for his own entrepreneurial enterprise and then for others seeking answers. It turned out that people were hungry to learn how to lead and Robert was poised to show them how!

On a muggy summer morning in 2021 I sat down with Robert over a cup of coffee. We were two of a kind. I am a former Naval officer who after twenty years went on to become involved in finance and business.

We were in sync. We completed each other's sentences and laughed at the same insights. We were both former special operators exchanging stories and helping each other with challenges and problems. Robert had a thriving business, this I knew. But he also had a young side gig he'd created to train organizations how to improve their leadership game. He called the course Elevate Your Leadership. I was intrigued to say the least. It was a perfect fit for Robert and the world as I knew it was certainly yearning for such training. After an hour of banter Robert grew quiet. "I have another project I've started to work on." I was curious. "A new project?" I asked. "Yes, I'm going to take the sum of all my leadership development wisdom and put it in a book." I smiled. "That, my friend, is a great idea!"

This book, *Elevate Your Leadership*, is the result of that dream in 2021. It is everything I thought it would be and more. A collection of examples, tips, tools, anecdotes, case studies, and yes, answers. It is packed full of information and knowledge, all from the direct leadership experience of Robert Pizzini, both in uniform and as a successful entrepreneur. The book is clear, concise, and inspirational at the same time. It is the encapsulation of all his wisdom and a reflection of the successful leadership course he has run for the last few years. Anybody – accomplished leaders, struggling leaders, and aspiring leaders – can benefit from reading *Elevate Your Leadership*. Take it from me, make an investment in yourself. Read this book. Take notes, go back, and read this book again. You will thank yourself for making the effort!

Marty Strong

CEO, Retried Navy SEAL

Author of *Be Nimble: How the Creative Navy SEAL Mindset Wins on the Battlefield and in Business*

and *Be Visionary: Strategic Leadership in the Age of Optimization*

GROUND RULES

I offer the following ground rules to assist you in grasping and applying the concepts put forth throughout this volume. Just like in hockey, chess, and political interactions, rules that are both written and unwritten—if followed—usually maximize gain. Please revisit these ground rules as necessary to ensure you are gaining the maximum value from this book.

1. Bottomline up front (**BLUF**).

BLUF is a military acronym which stands for "bottom line up front." **BLUF** creates speed and clarity in written communications such as email. **BLUF** means putting the most important details first. Don't delay your main point. Brevity provides clarity and saves time. Each chapter will begin with a **BLUF**.

2. Build and check your leadership foundation regularly.

Highly effective, long-lasting leaders have a foundation. Stability for a skyscraper requires a foundation that is both deep and wide and is largely unseen by others. Similarly, confident and effective leaders have a deliberate foundation. Neglecting your foundation makes you vulnerable. I have seen leaders go through periods of erosion and decline, and I have detected and repaired cracks in my foundation at times. If you do not have a deliberate foundation in your approach to leadership, we will build one throughout this book. If you do have a foundation, we will evolve it, which leads me to ground rule number three.

3. Surrender your ego.

It has been my experience that the best leaders check their ego at the door. They are open to new experiences and realize that everyone inside and outside of their organization brings value and can likely enlighten the leader in some way. Effective leaders seek this enlightenment. In releasing your ego, you are free to consider all ideas from everyone in your sphere.

4. Let the magic happen.

If you want to learn, you will. Effective leaders are open to new concepts and appreciate that it is important to build personal and professional habits that protect and preserve their leadership foundation. One of the goals of this book is to provide you with the practical guidance to build foundational leadership skills into daily routines. The awakening will happen as you turn each page, but the realization—the return on your investment—will accrue over time, ideally for the rest of your life.

5. Apply these concepts internally and externally.

We are viewed as leaders from a 360-degree perspective. My intent is that you have fun while reading, reviewing, and discussing the content of this book with your peers. The concepts that I discuss throughout this book should have meaning in all aspects of your life, not just your professional life. (Also see #10.)

6. Avoid polarized thinking.

There is no single, *right* way, to implement the leadership concepts that lie ahead. You will find what works for you and *your* team. Many social media posts quote big thinkers or famed leaders who employ absolutes such as Simon Sinek's: "Leadership is not about being in charge. Leadership is about taking care of those in our charge." I have read two of Simon Sinek's books and believe strongly in his teachings, but, I do not subscribe to absolute statements like the one above. Leadership is certainly about taking care of those in our charge, but it is *also* certainly about being in charge. When you are in charge, you must reflect on your responsibilities regularly. Avoid absolutes. The truth usually lies somewhere in the middle.

7. Get outside your comfort zone and your comfort zone will expand.

Try new things. Have fun experimenting with the principles presented here. Trust in the process. For example, when I say hydration is important, trust me. See if you feel more energized, make healthier food choices, exercise better and recover faster, not to mention have greater mental clarity.

8. Own your brand.

Well-developed leadership is a very personal brand, one which will likely be different than mine. In fact, it *should* be different. Your personal brand will be honed by your own experiences, and how they affected your growth. We remember our favorite coaches from our youth sports days as well as the coaches that made us not want to return for the next season. Same for our schoolteachers. We remember the good leaders that we worked for, as well as the not-so-good. As you reflect on these experiences, you will advance your leadership brand.

9. Mono, Stereo, and 5.1 Surround Sound

In addition to building your leadership skills and personal brand, this book is designed to help you develop current and future leaders on your team. In *mono* sound you consider how the principles in this book apply to you. In *stereo* sound you consider how these principles apply to those you lead, or the person sitting across the table from you, and in *5.1 surround* sound you will develop leaders and influence activity outside of your work setting. Everyone in your professional and personal spheres of influence will benefit from your investment in this process. I will refer to mono, stereo and surround sound throughout the book.

10. DRILL.

Remember use it or lose it? This book is designed with that end in mind: to help you *actually use* what you learn in each chapter. Each chapter ends with a drill, an opportunity to integrate what has been presented into your daily life.

One final thought before proceeding: the commander's intent is the overall goal of the mission, carried out by strategy, operations, and tactics. As commander of this mission, my intent is to:

Advance your ability to lead with confidence, competence, and energy while developing and leading a high performing team.

Last ground rule: **Have fun!**

INTRODUCTION

Before we dive into chapter one, we need to rewind a bit to my foundation, and I will ask you to do the same as we progress. Why? This book guides you through the deliberate actions which create a solid foundation for leadership, but the cornerstones of your foundation were laid long ago, during childhood. Your formative years contribute to your emerging leadership traits. I hope that my story, and the leadership lessons in this book, combine to deliver great value to you, the reader. Whether you are a leader now or aspire to be one someday, this book will guide you on your personal and professional journey to excellence.

In November of 1965, my father was attending law school at the University of Wisconson - Madison. As the state capital, Madison was a bustling center of commerce and politics. I was born just as my father was finishing his studies there. In 1966, upon his completion of law school and passing the bar exam, my mom and dad decided to set up their new family in the small town of Black River Falls, Wisconsin. Me, my parents, and my older brother lived in a small, three-bedroom house on Monroe Street, right next to the town's only golf course. It wasn't long before my baby sister was born, the year was 1970.

By October of 1970, at the age of thirty, my father was becoming a successful attorney. Like any young family, he and my mother had dreams and goals. Their life plan was on track, until he was tragically killed in a car accident. My father and my Uncle Joe were returning from dinner in a heavy rainstorm when my father lost control of his new 1969 Corvette Stingray sports car. My uncle suffered only a broken arm from the accident, but my father was gone forever. I was only four years old when my father died, but I still have limited memories of him. For example, I clearly remember taking his fancy new corvette to the car wash. I also remember going to the drive-in burger stand in our other car, a gold Oldsmobile. That sedan seemed like it was sixty-two feet long to me at the time.

Like most men in Wisconsin, my father was a sportsman. I recall taking our small fishing boat on trips to the lake in the summer and snowmobiling on trails through the woods in the winter. My playmates and I would form binoculars with our hands to spot pretend deer in the large field across the street from our home as our fathers butchered real deer in the garage. We hunted all sorts of imagined wildlife with our toy rifles that fired cork bullets.

I also remember fragments of my father's funeral. I recall my mom grasping my father's hand one last time in a church that was packed to standing-room only and overflowing outside. In addition to my father's obituary, the local newspaper printed a follow-on personal profile of my father titled "Dan Pizzini, A Great Guy to Know." Years later my mom told me that at the funeral, when I realized that my father would not wake up, I offered to get my drum and hit as hard as I could because weeks before his death, I'd used that drum to wake him up from a deep sleep.

My twenty-nine-year-old mother now faced a challenge that was not only completely unexpected, it was also untimely. She had to figure out how to run the household solo while raising the three of us kids. My sister was only four months old. Mom soon decided to move us back to Kenosha, Wisconsin where she and my father grew up and were married. Kenosha was also where both extended families lived.

Kenosha sits directly between Chicago, Illinois and Milwaukee, Wisconsin. It takes forty-five-minutes to drive from Kenosha to The Milwaukee Zoo and to Chicago's Museum of Science and Industry. The population of Kenosha in 1970 was 79,000. It was 90,000 when I left in 1984 and now hovers around 99,000. American Motors Corporation (AMC), and corner taverns were the two major industries. As I write this, AMC has long since shut down but the taverns remain. I recall a great blend of Italian, Polish, French, and German neighborhoods, and the festivals associated with those ethic groups. My early childhood certainly shaped me. It forged my basic sense of values and imprinted on me the point that life has a way of tripping you up in the most unexpected ways. The influence of my mom and extended family and memories of my father's strength and kindness all combined to guide me to the profession I eventually chose when I graduated from high school, the United States Navy.

Growing up in the 1970s and 1980s was far different from growing up today. The world was different, and our country was different too. This was a time in our history when no one used seat belts, hair bands ruled the radio waves, and cigarette smoking was everywhere. My high school even had a special smoking section. I saw the birth of Music Television, MTV, showcasing the song *Video Killed the Radio Star*, in 1981, along with the release of the hit *Hey Mickey*, (if you are my age you still remember the infectious chorus). The introduction of cable TV enabled MTV and hundreds of other cable channels to enter our homes.

Video games consumed a lot of my time and quarters. In those days we went to an arcade to play. Dining entertainment for kids was born when the first Chuck E. Cheese restaurant was launched in 1977 by Nolan Bushnell, co-founder of the video game maker, Atari. The restaurant was designed around kids and featured anatomical robot bands with Elvis, center stage. Think of an experience like Dave and Busters and Top Golf today.

Giant shopping malls were developed in the 1980s, quickly spreading across the US. The advent of food courts in these sprawling mega stores meant that families could shop, carb load, and shop some more while us teenagers "hung out" at the mall. I remember trying my first Orange Julius drink at the Hawthorn Mall in Vernon Hills Illinois. I also remember parachute pants, the silliness of the Cabbage Patch Doll, and the ingenuity of the Rubik's Cube. The world was exciting and constantly changing, keeping parents and kids alike, engaged and enthralled. From 1981-1989, Ronald Reagan served as the 40th President of the US. The movie *The Blues Brothers* debuted in 1980, and then in 1982 the iconic movie *Fast Times at Ridgemont High,* hit the movie screens accurately portraying the ups and downs of life as a teenager in the United States.

For most of us, our first exposure to leadership is through our parents. In addition to the love parents have for their children, parents lead us throughout our childhood, and beyond. They help us establish and accomplish objectives. They guide us as we attend school, participate in sports, and they lead us in faith. Growing up without a father is something that I was largely, but not completely, unaware of because I was so young when he left us so suddenly. My sister was too young to even remember our father. Neither of us knew what dad was really like.

I believe in many ways my father's death and the transition to a single parent family was more difficult for my older brother. He was seven at the time of the accident and had established a memorable relationship with our father. We all attended elementary school at Saint Mark's Catholic School in Kenosha. Later, I completed one year at Saint Joseph's High School before moving to Tremper High School. I played several sports including hockey, tennis, football, wrestling, baseball, and basketball. My brother and I excelled at every sport we played. As a result of my school and sports engagement I was in direct contact with many positive male role models. Role models that, for better or worse, partially filled in the absence of a father in my life.

My mom did not remarry until 1983, when I was a junior in high school. On Valentine's Day in 1982, when I was sixteen, my mom was diagnosed with breast cancer. The treatment for breast cancer in the1980s was nowhere near as advanced as it is today. Although I did not fully realize it at the time, mom's cancer was serious. Thankfully, she made a full recovery and today lives in Jefferson Wisconsin just across the street from my younger sister and her family. Because of my mom's cancer, my sister eventually became an oncology nurse. I firmly believe that the resilience me and my siblings developed over the years was always in our DNA, inherited from our mother, who became a widow for the second time in 2015.

Growing up playing hockey, each year we attended a hockey banquet held at the Italian American Club on fifty-second street in Kenosha. Throughout our years participating in youth hockey my brother and I were both selected for MVP and Sportsmanship awards. This was decades before the "everyone gets a trophy" era in youth sports. In my case, stitches, concussions, and a fractured shoulder were among the injuries I sustained during junior high and high school.

I also became a certified scuba diver at the age of 12. I was enamored with The Undersea World of Jacques Cousteau. I watched in black and white, and eventually in what was then called technicolor, as Cousteau and his team of aquanauts explored the oceans of the world. Captain Cousteau and his team were making technological advances in scuba (self-contained underwater breathing apparatus) diving equipment and procedures. At the same time, treasure hunters were making significant discoveries of sunken gold- and silver-laden Spanish galleons such as the wreck of the Nuestra Señora de Atocha. Famed treasure hunter Mel Fisher discovered the wreck of the Atocha in 1985. The ship was sunk by a hurricane in 1622, in twenty-five feet of water off the coast of Key West, Florida.

At the age of 12, I went to Water World, Kenosha's local scuba dive shop, to purchase my first diving mask. I believe the cost was around $20, which was a lot of money to a 12-year-old. The owner of the dive shop was sweeping the floor at the time. I offered to sweep the floor in exchange for a discount on that $20 mask, and to my great surprise, he agreed. Working at Water World was my first job, which lasted throughout high school.

Water World was a magical place. Jim, the dive shop owner, became a surrogate father. In addition to being a scuba diving and flight instructor, Jim had energy, intelligence, and was a great teacher. My duties included retail, rental, filling high pressure scuba tanks, and organizing dive trips to Florida each winter, and I loved every bit of it, even though my official title was Slave One. I learned how to scuba dive in the many small lakes across the state of Wisconsin as well as enjoying many wonderful dives in Lake Michigan. The discussions that we had on the drive to the various lakes are reminiscent of the conversations I've had with my son and daughter over the years.

I dove on a shipwreck for the first time at the age of 13. The wreck of the *Prins Willem V*, also known as The Willie, sank on October 14, 1954, three miles off the coast of Milwaukee in 90 feet of water after colliding with the towing cables of a barge. The *Willie* remains the most visited shipwreck in Wisconsin. The wreck of the ship *Wisconsin* was my second wreck dive. The *Wisconsin* was an iron-hulled package steamer built in 1881 that sank off the coast of Kenosha, on 29 October 1929, while enroute from Chicago to Milwaukee. I lived on 2nd avenue, just one block from Lake Michigan, so the *Wisconsin* lay in 90-130 feet of water, 6.5 miles south-southeast from where I grew up. In 2009, this shipwreck site was added to the National Register of Historic Places. While in the eighth grade, I was scuba diving in Pearl Lake, located in Rockford Illinois. During this dive I encountered a mask squeeze, a type of facial barotrauma injury that occurs most commonly while scuba diving or freediving. This condition occurs when divers fail to equalize the pressure in their face mask with the surrounding water pressure as they descend. Although the symptoms of this condition appear significant (my eyes were black and blue, and the whites of my eyes filled with blood), it is not a truly serious medical condition, and it heals quickly. My eighth-grade classmates were shocked by my appearance, which I attempted to hide with sunglasses, irritating the teachers and nuns at St. Mark's school.

The Florida trips included diving at the John Pennekamp Coral Reef State Park, located on Key Largo in Florida. The park includes approximately 70 nautical square miles of adjacent Atlantic Ocean waters, filled with coral reefs. We also dove the freshwater springs and underwater caves of the Ichetucknee River. We dove with alligators in the Rainbow River, and we dove with the manatees in the Crystal River. Scuba diving and commercial diving intrigued and stimulated me, and I knew in my gut that I wanted to dive for a living.

However, at this point in my life, growing up without a father was negatively impacting my decision-making. During my sophomore year in high school I became so involved with scuba diving that I regrettably gave up participation in all organized sports. I attended commercial diver training while I was in my senior year of high school and began to have thoughts of becoming a US Navy Deep Sea Diver.

My love of all things diving and the need for a more regimented and disciplined lifestyle made the idea of joining the United States Navy quite appealing. Perhaps by divine intervention, The Tremper High

School library had a book entitled *Navy Diver: The Incredible Undersea Adventures of a Master Diver* by Joseph Sidney Karneke & Victor Boesen. After reading this book, I was convinced that it was my destiny to become a Navy Diver.

One of my high school friends, Joe, had an older brother, Jeff, who enlisted in the Navy several months before my reading of *Navy Diver*. During my senior year I recall Jeff coming home on leave after completing Navy boot camp wearing his dress blue uniform. It was at this moment that I made the decision that would change my life forever. I took one look at that sharp uniform, and Jeff's new sense of confidence and poise, and went straight to the local Navy recruiting office. I didn't go alone. My friend Joe had decided it was time for him to take the leap, too. As we walked into the recruiting center, we split up: I went in to see the Navy recruiter and Joe went to the Marine recruiter's office. We enlisted on that day under what was called the delayed entry program. This program allowed people to join the military early, before attaining the minimum age of seventeen. You were obligated to join as soon as you graduated high school and reached that minimum age. Once you checked off on these requirements you were off to boot camp!

Although I was not a stellar student in high school, I scored remarkably high on the Armed Services Vocational Aptitude Battery, simply known as the ASVAB. This is the test that every military enlistee takes to determine which professions within the military one may qualify for. While I was aware of the testing requirements for Navy Diver, which I exceeded, little did I know at the time that I also scored high enough to apply to Explosive Ordnance Disposal (EOD) school (think disarming bombs), or even nuclear propulsion. I had no interest in these other areas despite my high aptitude scores. I wanted to be a diver! In 1984 I graduated high school and reported to Navy camp boot in San Diego, California. My new journey was just beginning.

The Navy SEALS were not as well known in the 1980s and I only learned of the SEALS while in boot camp. My first exposure came as a tough-as-nails SEAL instructor administered the physical training (PT) test for all Diver, EOD, and SEAL candidates. The PT test began with a timed five-hundred-yard swim, followed by push-ups, sit-ups, and pull-ups, ending with a timed mile –and-a-half run. There were about 30 people in my group. Ten of us made the swim within the time limit. Most of the candidates didn't make it through the first three laps in the swimming pool. More candidates fell out during the push-ups, sit-ups, and pull-ups, and in the end five of us made the mile and a half run within the prescribed time. The Vietnam-era SEAL who administered the test congratulated us and sent us to the reclassification office to have orders written. My life's dream was now in motion.

Having successfully completed the PT test, I was on my way to US Navy Diver training, or so I thought. The final step to receive orders was the physical examination, which included a vision test. While my test for color blindness was easily within standards, my binocular visual acuity was not, and in an instant, my dream was crushed. I left that eye exam with tears in my eyes, still determined to become a Navy Diver.

This would prove to be just one of many obstacles which seemed insurmountable at the time. However, staying open to new opportunities and never giving up on a goal are recurrent themes in my military and professional experience. As we will discuss next, setting your personal and professional cardinal directions are part of building your foundation as a leader.

PART I: THE ART OF LEADERSHIP

BLUF: Conduct an intelligence preparation of the battlefield (IPB)

Before we dive deep into Part 1, The Art of Leadership, it is important to establish an intelligence preparation of the business landscape, the strategic landscape—what challenges modern leaders face with employee expectations, changes in organizational structure with more matrixed teams, more remote workplaces, and employee engagement at an all-time low. It is vital that you understand the terrain into which you are heading. Chapter one situates the ground truth that modern leaders face.

With this in mind, we move into describing the art of leadership. This has been defined in many ways, but modern leadership requires not only a strong sense of personal brand and mission but also entails the capacity to harness many forces—from economic and cultural pressures to shifts in predominant technology and communications platforms—in order to exert influence. Ultimately, you must persuade your employees and clients to invest in your way of doing things, either through time and sweat, or by purchasing your products or services.

Leadership, among it's many definitions, includes the art of persuasion. In Chapter 2, I share a bit of my own professional and personal achievements, and challenges—the moments which have informed and defined who I am today. In Chapter 3 we define "art" and discuss various definitions of leadership, while providing the foundation for you to begin to define leadership in your own words, then, in Chapter 4 you will finalize and take ownership of your leadership brand. In Chapter 5 we dissect various misconceptions of leadership concepts. We close Part 1 in Chapter 6 with a probing discussion of one of the most pressing leadership challenges of today: diversity, equity and inclusion.

CHAPTER 1: THE CHALLENGE OF MODERN LEADERSHIP

BLUF: You Must Understand the Strategic Landscape

The Ground Truth

In military special operations, we try to determine the ground truth in differing Areas of Operation (AOR). We also observe and identify the political, social, and cultural atmospherics, which help establish the ground truth. The ground truth in today's workforce is that the vast majority are Millennials who do not expect to remain in their current job for more than two years. Long-term employment with the same company for 30 years is no longer the norm. Millennials want their careers to have a purpose, they want to use their knowledge, skills, and abilities, and they value work-life balance. Employee engagement and productivity are at all-time lows. Today's leader faces many challenges. The modern leader should take time to survey the strategic landscape, as we will do in this chapter.

In its third iteration, the Gallup, Inc., *State of the American Workplace* report (2018) was conducted among more than 195,000 employees. This report found that only a third of all employees are actively engaged in their work and 16% are disengaged from their responsibilities, undoing what the engaged employees are creating. Half reported that they were actively looking for a new position. Compared to international benchmarks, the American worker is only half as engaged as international counterparts.

- 51% of workers are looking to leave their current job
- 47% would leave for their ideal job, even if it meant less pay
- 44% of Millennials (born 1981-1996) plan on leaving their current job within two years
- 74% of workers are satisfied with their current job

- 1 in 3 employees changed jobs in the previous year, and 91% of these left their company to do so
- 68% of employees report that they are overqualified

According to Gallup, these four factors drive employee retention:

- Career growth
- Pay and benefits
- Management
- Culture and values

Complimenting the Gallup study is the 2019 Glassdoor Economic Research survey of factors that matter most in the workplace. Please take a moment here, and rank the following workplace factors in your order of importance:

___Pay and Compensation

___Work Life Balance

___Business Outlook

___Career Opportunities

___Senior Leadership

___Culture and Values

Now let's look at the Glassdoor results. How did your ranking compare to the below graph?

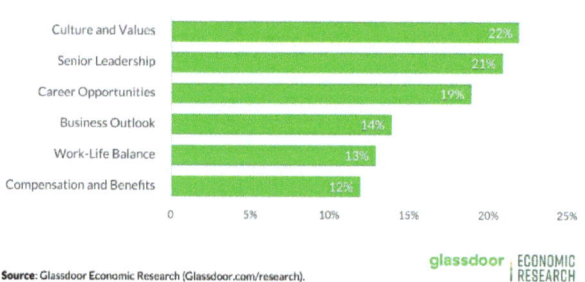

The graphic above from the 2019 Glass Door Survey indicates that Culture and Values is the strongest predictor of employee satisfaction in the US, UK, France, Canada, and Germany. The same survey found that 77% of adults would consider a company's culture before applying for a job, and 56% reported that they value culture more than salary. Culture and Values in the workplace matter more to U.S. workers than all other categories including pay and compensation.

What enables culture and values? Take a look at the second item down on the bar chart...senior leadership, again, this is consistent across five developed countries. The executive team and the senior leaders within any organization enable culture and values, or at least they should. If your culture and values are lower, turnover will be higher. I have learned this lesson from all perspectives, from being the newest member of a team to owning a multimillion-dollar business.

Culture and values are enabled from the top down and owned from the bottom up. Said another way, the most effective leaders enable high culture and model high values, but each teammate must genuinely feel ownership and make positive contributions to the culture.

Leaders need teammates who want to show up every day and do a great job. Anything less is not good for the organization or the individual. If those you lead are excited to come to work every day, the potential for success is high. If, on the other hand, members of your team have a lack of energy or are compliant rather than committed, the potential for success is reduced, or even sabotaged.

Components of a thriving culture include:

- everyone having a voice
- a sense of meaningful contribution to the company's mission
- pride in the company's mission
- recognition as a subject matter expert
- promotion opportunities
- a genuine concern for the well-being and success of all teammates.

There are many more components of a thriving culture depending on the mission of the organization. We all should be in it for the long haul. If leaders focus on culture and values, the long haul will be longer, return on investment (ROI) will be notably higher, and teammate engagement will be personally and professionally more rewarding.

Let us go back to the Glassdoor survey results to enhance our situational awareness regarding the strategic landscape. How did you rank the six items in the survey? Your responses likely aligned with how long you have been in your current position, with your current organization, and in the workforce at large. Newer members of the workforce would rank pay and compensation higher, but among those who have several years in professional life, one can easily understand how culture and values, as well as senior leadership, become the factors that matter most. We want to sleep easy at night and not let workplace distractions interfere with our personal and professional lives. Confidence in good culture and values at work positively impacts our lives when we are not at work. Penna's model of hierarchical engagement may account for changing priorities. Someone just entering the workforce and looking to make ends meet will certainly give pay and compensation a higher priority. As young professionals gain experience and expertise, their rankings will change.

Penna's Hierarchical Model of Engagement

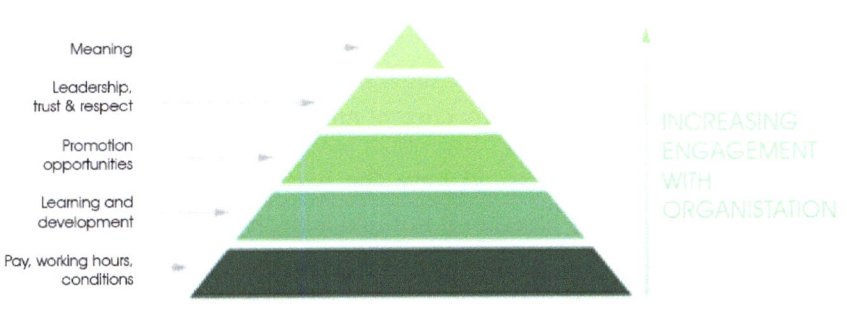

What does this suggest for the modern leader? To be effective working in this environment, it is imperative to take stock of the landscape in ways previous leaders may not have, when top-down directives were more customary, and employees were more compliant. To lead today requires a different set of instruments. You can try to be a modern leader, but without understanding the ground truth, you're not leading, and you risk losing your teammates who are on the move, looking for high culture and values in the workplace.

Fully engaged employees will contribute more to your organization's success, and *your* ability to help them find meaning and purpose in their work will encourage them to stay. Retention is possible, but you must be intentional in your actions to create a thriving workplace which satisfies Penna's hierarchy of engagement. Only 1 in 5 employees feels that they are led in a way that motivates them to do their best and contribute to the organization. Nearly all (91%) said they had to leave the company for their next position, suggesting that the leadership team did not do a good job providing a path for growth within the organization.

Another critical factor is the hyper-connected nature of social media. Most jobs are found through a network of relationships, and that network has never been easier to access. Freelancers have several platforms they can use to build a side hustle, and employees may choose to leave once a side hustle shows promise. The conscious leader must spot this "ground truth" and adapt. This network can also be powerful to your organization as most new hires in today's workforce come from personal referrals by current employees.

I never imagined that I would have the luxury of contemplating a position on the basis of whether it fulfilled a larger mission or purpose, but upon reflection, my military career certainly fits this concept, as does my current situation, including the writing of this book. However, today's landscape has changed. When workers were asked what attributes they would consider most strongly when evaluating a new position, which would you imagine were most important from among these choices?

1. The ability to do what they do best.
2. Greater work-life balance and better personal well-being
3. Greater stability and job security
4. A significant increase in income
5. The opportunity to work for a company with a great brand or reputation

Sixty percent of employees responded that doing what they do best is most important. This response rate was consistent across age and gender, and is a considerable factor in creating and advancing a positive culture. Throughout my military career, myself and my teammates wanted to be very good at our craft, so this is not an "a-ha" moment from my perspective, but I also know what it is like to not be properly challenged and engaged by my leaders, and it can be deenergizing to say the least. Engaged employees are less likely to leave. Employees want to contribute and be recognized as experts or as very good at what they do. As leaders, hiring and retaining top talent is one of our core competencies. Creating a culture that values teammate contributions to the mission will help prevent our top talent from seeking high culture and values elsewhere.

Most private sector small to medium size businesses face a unique challenge in that leadership development is not considered until it is long overdue, and larger organizations fail to modernize leadership development. This creates frustration and contributes to valued teammates looking to move on. In the military, the typical soldier, sailor, airman, or marine has already held two or three leadership positions by age 25 and attended several leadership training events. Civilian careers need to build momentum and offer growth opportunities as well.

Your teammates should face challenges that require the development of creative solutions, some of which will have an inherent risk. Failure is inevitable along the way, which can provide unique and extremely valuable learning experiences for your organization, or they can destroy a team, depending on how leaders react.

Regardless of what your leadership role is, you are relied upon to make good decisions that are in the best interest of your organization, your teammates, and yourself, in that order. In the Navy we say ship, shipmates, self.

Within my organization I deliver an annual strategy in the form of a quad chart. A quad chart is a military-style document with four sections that rely on each other to deliver a complete message. The first section of my strategy quad chart has our Mission, Vision, and Values.

Mission

We bring people together through the dream of flight

Vision

Our vision is to lead the industry nationally and internationally in the amusement, recreation, and sport of indoor skydiving. Through focused leadership and teamwork, we will innovate and evolve to enhance our growth, vitality, and contributions to community.

Values

Loyalty - Integrity - Professionalism

Motto

Excellence In All We Do

The next section is Culture. My current strategic vision lists six items in the Culture quadrant, all developed or influenced by input from the entire team. While Mission, Vision, and Values are unlikely to change, the culture section not only *can* change, but I *encourage* changes as the team dynamic tends to evolve over time. By seeking input from your team and enabling their ideas, you are leading in a way that creates ownership for all.

Culture

- Give to others through mentorship, leadership, and motivation
- Develop and advance professional growth of all our staff
- Promote/Enable a mindset of physical fitness, mental health and wellness
- Believe in yourself and your teammates
- Recognize and create opportunities
- Encourage creative thinking to advance individual and company objectives

Section three takes us to:

Focus Areas

- Strengthen consumer awareness regarding our full range of offerings to include STEM, All Abilities, Membership, Youth League, Leadership Development and Team Building, Corporate Outings, LIFT 1 and 2
- Create Sales and Marketing campaigns leveraging the latest technology and mainstream trends

- Fill the weekends
- Lead the wind tunnel industry in advancing business processes, military training, staff professional development, and Flight Instructor training
- Grow business across all revenue streams by increasing manifested time, retail, upsells, and programs

The fourth and final section of the quad chart contains measurable Key performance Indicators (KPIs)

Goals

- Exceed 2022 projections
- Grow group sales through STEM, Birthdays, and Elevate Your Leadership
- Advance funding for Seatack Soars (an after school program that we currently sponsor, and want to expand through charitable partners)
- Grow membership and increase member flight time through objective data analysis
- Attract and retain talented and dedicated teammates

This one-page strategic vision gives each team member something to strive for and helps keep everyone synchronized and moving in the same cardinal direction, further contributing to a positive and inclusive culture.

My friend and retired Navy SEAL Captain Ryan Croley seeks alignment among all teammates. In our podcast discussion, Ryan discusses how minor deviations are not an issue and sometimes lead to discovery, but if the team gets too far out of alignment, then the leader must course correct. Alignment among all teammates contributes significantly to a positive culture. Alignment also will result in a higher degree of trust among all teammates. A high level of trust throughout any organization is the golden ticket.

With high trust we attack issues and not each other.

This is how your business can grow from surviving to thriving. Build great culture and values which develops a high level of trust, and everyone focuses on the mission. Water cooler distractions and time wasted on non-product or service-related issues is reduced or eliminated. I want to emphasize here that while this may sound theoretical, I am speaking from firsthand experience and deliberate experimentation within my business. Leadership is not rocket science but developing authentic trust is critical to forging a high-performing team, and it takes time.

The three levels of warfare…and business

Modern military theory divides war into strategic, operational, and tactical levels. Although this division has its basis in the Napoleonic Wars and the American Civil War, modern theory regarding these three levels was formulated by the Prussians following the Franco-Prussian War.

Strategic Level: The strategic level focuses on defining and supporting national policy and relates directly to the outcome of a war or other conflict as a whole.

Operational Level: The operational level is concerned with employing military forces in a theater of war or theater of operations to obtain an advantage over the enemy and thereby attain strategic goals through the design, organization, and conduct of campaigns and major operations.

Tactical Level: In the traditional sense, the various operations that make up a campaign are themselves made up of maneuvers, engagements, and battles.

As a leader within the private sector industry, I noticed significant similarity in that there are three levels of business that perfectly align with the three levels of warfare.

Strategic Level: CEO, board of directors, executive team and other stake holders define, develop, and support corporate strategy as it relates to ROI. People at the strategic level in business often worked their way up through the ranks just as strategic level leaders in the military…but…not always, and this is a key difference. Strategic level decision-makers in the private sector who do not possess the technical knowledge and have not experienced adequate leadership development will have great difficulty understanding their role as the leader of the organization, and often say and do things that are inappropriate. They can set policy or business objectives on the wrong course, alienate customers, and fracture trust.

Operational Level: The operational level is concerned with employing management level leaders, vice presidents for example, who develop processes such as sales marketing campaigns, target audiences, manufacturing systems, organizational architecture (structures), budgets, innovation and modernization to achieve ROI. This level of business also provides all necessary manpower, training, and equipment for tactical level execution. Operational level leaders are authorized to make course corrections within pre-approved guidelines for a variety of situations.

Tactical level: In business, your customer-facing teammates represent the tactical level. They deliver the product or service as their primary role within the company. Your tactical level teammates represent the business as much, or more, than at the operational and strategic levels. Your tactical level crew can easily bring great credit upon the organization, or they can create havoc.

It is critical that everyone on the team understands these three levels of business and where each person resides. It is not uncommon for all team members to interact with people one level above and below their officially assigned position. By design, the operational level bridges the intent of strategy to the execution of tactics, and—in turn—successful tactical execution results in realizing strategic goals.

As your team develops under your leadership, another construct that may help you gain clarity on where your teammates are and where you are leading them toward is the Collins Five Levels of Leadership. This model is a great tool to help you develop your people by determining where they are in the architecture, and where they aspire to ascend.

The following graphic depicts the relationship between Jim Collins' Level 5 Leadership, and the strategic, operational, and tactical levels of warfare. In the diagram below, Levels 1 and 2 align with the Tactical level of warfare; Levels 3 and 4 align with the Operational level of warfare, and Level 5 is the Strategic level of warfare.

I hesitated to present the graphic as it looks like a painful eye chart at first glance, however, building on the above discussion, we see clearly the overlapping interactions across all levels of the organization. Notice that Collins' levels 3 and 4 align with the military Operational level. This is a vital hinge between tactical and strategic levels.

At the level 3-4 junction—the epicenter of any organization and the analog bridging the tactical to the strategic,—you should ensure you have highly experienced, trained, and educated people. These mid-level operatives have (hopefully) institutional memory about what has worked and what hasn't, have a good sense of your organization's culture on the front lines, and can synthesize signals into a coherent message to feed to the CEO.

Placing good people at this vital hinge means your CEO should not be routinely bogged down at the tactical and operational levels. While some CEOs like to be "hands-on," this can impede the leader's ability to think strategically. To ensure the CEO is equipped to make sound strategic decisions, information should be curated as it is conveyed from tactical through operational to the strategic level of command.

By considering the needs of the individual via the Penna model and the needs of the team via the Collins model, you as a leader will know when and where your influence is needed, and when and where it is not.

External factors: social and political landscape

As I close this survey of the challenges presented to modern leaders, I would be remiss if I did not discuss factors external to the organization, such as social and political movements. While I have seen many organizations jump on the bandwagon of the day, my approach for business is to stick to matters of business. As I write this book, the social and political landscape is more polarized than I have ever seen. Woke and cancel culture seem to be the soup of the day for some businesses, large and small. Some on my team want me to take a more proactive stand regarding what they consider to be social injustice. After a year of civil unrest in Portland, Seattle, and other U.S. cities, local businesses and the individuals who work for those businesses have suffered greatly. In focusing on business operations, executives must ensure sustained profitability and not let emotion cloud their judgement. Thus, Chapter Six is dedicated to evaluating the social and cultural landscape with respect to Diversity, Equity and Inclusion (DE&I) as I believe it is a critical factor in developing a meaningful corporate culture through inclusivity.

Developing your corporate culture must be done with clear intention and good communication, or you risk being perceived as susceptible to the cultural whims of the day. For example, Major League Baseball moved the All Star game from Atlanta to Denver. The fallout from this highly political statement has yet to be realized. If you propel your organization forth as a warrior for the social and political movements of the day you will likely alienate some on your team and some within your customer base, potentially impacting your organizational cohesion, and your financial viability.

On the other hand, you may have teammates who are social justice warriors and want you to use your business to advance their personal initiatives. If you choose not to take on specific initiatives, some may lose faith. As time goes on, your steadfast support of core values will pay dividends, ultimately increasing trust and cohesion, while preserving the opportunity for teammates to bring significant social and cultural issues to your attention. As we will discuss in Chapter 6 more fully, conversation leads to clarity and it is important to foster a culture that allows for conversation. It may not always lead to action or complete resolution, but your team will value the opportunity to have an open conversation.

What can you ascertain from this information? How can you use this information to advance the initiatives of your organization?

The post-COVID workplace remains the same as the pre-covid workplace regarding the importance and impact of culture and values. Again, I say this because I am living it with my entire team. We endured throughout the fog of COVID and prevailed as the fog began to lift. We wanted to remain together as a team. We wanted each other to succeed. While teammates in my organization come and go due mainly to school, we did lose one person who was more committed to social justice initiatives than to the good of the organization, and the team.

I am going to close this chapter with a sea story. I am a sailor, and sailors love to tell sea stories, although this one takes place on land. On March 23, 2020 Governor Northam of Virginia ordered all businesses to close to the public due to the COVID-19 pandemic. After assembling my leadership team to consider all the possible scenarios, we decided to use all operating funds to make payroll for the next three weeks. This was before the payroll Protection Plan and the CARES act were in place, but it was after the generous unemployment had been announced. We assembled everyone in the company and offered full pay to stay home for three weeks, using every operating dollar to make payroll, as long as they stayed with the team and did not take the unemployment, while we waited for the fog of the pandemic to lift. All but one person agreed.

The reasoning here was that if everyone left for the easy money, we would have to rehire and retrain before we could reopen, which creates difficulty upon reopening and regaining the momentum we need to operate safely and efficiently, and generate good margins. I contacted my banker to indicate that I would not be making the April 1st loan payment. After some back and forth, he agreed to talk with people on his end and get back to me. Certainly, I was not the only business owner to call with this dilemma. No income means no loan payment, plain and simple. By the end of the day he called to indicate that yes, this is a big problem for many in their book of business, and he would defer the principal component of my loan, but the interest was still due. Now, I fully understand that interest never sleeps, but no income is no income, and I had to convince him to defer the interest as well. By the next day, the scope of the issue was much clearer to bankers across the country, and both my principal and interest were deferred for an initial period of three months. With a fully trained staff at home and ready to return to work, I thought we were in good shape, relatively speaking. The gamble paid off, so to speak.

We conduct a significant amount of military training for military freefall parachuting. Three weeks into the pandemic the military contacted us and indicated that we were key and essential to their training, especially since travel was heavily restricted, and they required us to be open per the terms of the contract. Up to this point, no one on my team had contracted COVID-19 and the protocols of social distancing, masking, hand washing, and a slew of other items were in place. I was personally confident that we could safely train the military and prevent transmission of SARS-CoV-2. Some government occupational health and safety folks visited us and unofficially determined given the volume of our wind generating system, with wind speeds in excess of 150 miles per hour, and the complete replacement of ambient air at a rate of over 100 times that of an operating room, the virus simply could not persist within our flight chamber. So, three weeks into the pandemic, we were operating at a high rate fulfilling our government contracts. By now the CARES act had been implemented, and the fog began to lift ever so slightly. Soon after the resumption of military training, we invited our members (sport and recreational tunnel flyers) to return. Given that they are experienced fliers and not the general public, we thought—correctly—that we could manage to COVID-19 protocols and safety while allowing them to fly.

Back to the banker. I want to be clear that I have always had a great relationship with my banker, and he flexed and adapted, big time, just as I did along with my entire team. Knowing that even though my principal and interest were deferred, I also know that interest never really sleeps. Given the unexpected return of our government clients, I was able to make all interest payments uninterrupted. Fast forward to June of 2020, and the phased reopening of our beaches welcomed enough summer tourists to float us back above the waterline, from a business perspective. Everyone on my team played a critical role in the decision-making process throughout the COVID-19 pandemic. The chapters that follow outline my approach to leadership and how this approach enabled my business to not only survive through the

COVID-19 crisis, but to thrive. Of our 7 years in business, 2021 was our best on record.

Now that we have an in-depth understanding of the strategic landscape—the factors that a leader confronts every day, both internally and externally, such as satisfying the human needs for engagement, a sense of fulfillment, purpose, the importance of culture, how each teammate views the workplace, and how you as the leader are the organizational architect—we can move to discussing the artistic aspects of great leadership.

DRILL:

1. Develop a Strategic Vision and update it every year.

2. Assess the culture within your organization and develop methods to improve it.

3. Develop a leadership continuum for yourself and others you lead and dedicate time and budget to an open and continuous leadership development pipeline.

CHAPTER 2: DEFINING MOMENTS

BLUF: Exploit your defining moments.

As I mentioned in the introduction, I grew up in Kenosha Wisconsin, which has unfortunately been in the news for the wrong reasons in 2020 and 2021. After enlisting in the US Navy in 1984, and successfully completing the Navy Diver PT test while in boot camp as described in the introduction, it was difficult for me to get assigned to US Navy Diver training, as my vision was disqualifying, or so I thought. The eye test I took in boot camp revealed that my eyesight was not strong enough to be a Navy Diver. I walked away from that exam with tears in my eyes and a determination to remedy this situation. My life's dream for the past three years was gone after a two-minute eye test.

A few months later, while I was attending advanced electronics training at the Naval Training Center, Great Lakes, Illinois, I took another eye test. The results of this test easily qualified me for diving duty, but now I was locked into a six-year electronics career. After taking the PT test again and easily passing it, I realized that the only way out of this electronics contract was to fail the written and practical exams, which would attract negative attention and threaten reclassification and orders to Navy Diver training. After some contemplation, I reaffirmed that I joined the Navy to be a deep-sea diver and would risk getting kicked out the Navy to make my dream come true. I failed out of the electronics school, and after a serious ass chewing, I was released from the electronics contract and sent to the Naval Submarine Training Center Pacific, where one of the Navy's four diver training centers was located, on Ford Island in the middle of Pearl Harbor, Hawaii.

As motivated as I was to be the best student the Navy had ever encountered, the environment was intimidating. I was surrounded by fellow sailors who had also met the academic testing requirements and the physical fitness standards just to be selected for Navy Diver training. Some were in better physical condition than me, and some were not. Some had college degrees, I did not. Several of my classmates were senior in rank to me as they had been in the Navy for a few years and had come from the fleet to dive school. I was still relatively new, and over the past year I attended schools only, and had no fleet experience. At Navy Dive School, the instructors not only build Navy Divers, they build teams. Being a great teammate is a key characteristic of the job. The process of building great teammates required the instructors to break down the individual through physical training and pool drills such as drown-proofing (floating motionless with ankles and wrists bound with rope), and rebuild a team-oriented Navy Diver. Of the 25 or so of us who began Navy Diver training in June of 1985, eleven of us graduated. There were two shipmates in particular that I thought would have no problem with the physical training and academic standards. One was a swimmer in college and looked like the stereotypical ripped California golden boy, and the other was a tough, but nice, guy from Boston, accent and all. Neither made it through pool week. Week four of training, called pool week, consisted of scuba diving in a large swimming pool. Throughout the week we would have to swim in our buddy pairs on the surface wearing twin 72 cubic feet, steel tanks. The air tanks were much heavier when full of air, making the surface swim challenging, especially if you were prone to leg cramps. After a 10 minute surface swim, we then descended to the bottom of the pool to receive "pool hits." Pool hits are a confidence building process where instructors attack dive buddy pairs by removing face masks and the scuba air supply while spinning and disorienting one or both divers and trying to separate each buddy pair. Successful students will breath hold, stay together, and remain calm throughout the hit and when the commotion is over, each diver, and each buddy pair, are required to recover and restore all equipment while remaining at the pool's bottom, in roughly 12 feet of water. The final test during pool week consists of students swimming around the perimeter of the bottom of the pool in buddy pairs while the instructors conduct pool hits and evaluate each candidate's ability to remain calm and fully recover from the hit. This phase of training proved to be too much for the college swimmer, the Boston native, and several others. When your air supply is taken away from you, even in only 12 feet of water depth, panic is the body's natural response, which leads undesirable outcomes. As I remained calm and successfully recovered from each hit throughout the week, my confidence grew.

My dive buddy and I passed pool week, and the remaining six weeks of learning about surface supplied dive systems and the training that followed. The final qualification dive was a 190-foot surface supplied air dive using the MK12 (Mark 12) surface supplied diving system (SSDS). The MK12 helmet, made of yellow fiberglass, with nickel plated bronze fittings, was a new and futuristic looking helmet with large glass view ports known as windows. While walking on the floor of the Pacific Ocean in 190 feet of crystal-clear sea water, I remember looking up through the top window of my MK12 helmet, towards the water's surface and seeing my teammates leaning over the side of the diving craft as they tended to my air hose. My dream was realized in June of 1985 when I graduated from class 85-20-2C, US Navy Second Class Diver training in Pearl Harbor Hawaii, at the age of 19. This continues to be one of the proudest moments of my life. I truly was part of something much bigger than myself and although I did not know it at the time, this was a defining moment in my life.

Second Class Diver training creates competent divers who are great teammates.

Two years into my Navy diving career I was selected for First Class (1C, which we call "one charlie") diver training in Panama City Florida. 1C

Divers learn the complexities of mixed gas surface supplied diving, surface decompression diving using air and oxygen, and hyperbaric treatment protocols for maladies of diving to include decompression sickness (the bends) and arterial gas embolism. 1C divers are also trained to supervise highly complex diving operations where many people are under your direct charge. 1C divers are trained to be leaders. During my four years as a 1C diver, I supervised hundreds of dives and began to deliberately build my leadership brand, one of unusually high competence for being relatively junior in the enlisted ranks. During this time I was exposed to EOD, and loved what I saw.

EOD consists of highly competent and capable teams operating complex equipment in austere locations while employing high explosives as a primary skill set. EOD Technicians attend schools that are highly classified, and most also attend college. I applied for EOD school in 1991 and was accepted into the training pipeline in 1992. For trainees not already dive qualified, EOD school is roughly 14 months in duration. There is no spring, summer, or winter break. EOD school is 10-12 hours per day including "extra study." Extra study is where an instructor will be available in the classroom, usually from 6-8 pm after a 10-hour day of PT, classroom, lab, and field training. If you fail a written or practical test and have no record of attending extra study, woe unto you. It's that simple. If, on the other hand, you were diligent in attending extra study and fell short on an exam or practical test, the instructors would give everything they had to help you succeed. This is leadership.

This is the kind of team I wanted to qualify for, contribute to, and ultimately lead.

EOD Technicians not only dive the world's oceans—US Navy Divers…We Explore the Ocean Floor—we also employ the mobility skills of parachute insertion from fixed wing aircraft, and fast rope or rappel insertion from helicopters. We also employ a very high-tech underwater breathing apparatus called the MK16, which is a bubbleless rebreathing apparatus with very a low magnetic signature necessary for locating and rendering safe sea mines. Navy EODs disarm (render safe) every type of explosive to include conventional, chemical, biological, radiological, and nuclear weapons, on land and under water. EOD teams deploy around the world to search for, locate, identify, and disable explosive devices of all types, from IEDs on the battlefields of Iraq and Afghanistan, to radiological and nuclear devices set by terrorists, to large sea mines designed to sink aircraft carriers. Navy EOD is everywhere around the world where these threats exist. The successful EOD trainee possesses intelligence, physical stamina, intellectual curiosity, and confidence—to the point of overconfidence at times—and a willingness to give their soul to their teammates, and country. Sadly, I have attended numerous funerals at Arlington National Cemetery in honor of Navy EOD Techs who did just that. They gave their country and their teammates their lives.

EOD school for me was challenging, but not to the point of great stress. I knew the amount of work necessary to be successful and I was more than willing to put in the hours. Understanding the characteristics of every type of explosive is a daunting task. Each explosive, and explosive device has unique characteristics that an EOD Tech must quickly recognize. For example, heat, shock, and friction are safety conditions that we do want to expose explosives to. For a magnetic-fired explosive device, we do not want to bring metallic objects near the device. All EOD techs must be able to positively identify every type of military and nonmilitary explosive device, conduct the proper render safe procedure, and dispose of (usually via high order detonation) the explosive material and associated fuses and firing devices, while collecting intelligence regarding the device and the people placing the device.

After completing EOD school in February of 1993, I was assigned to EOD MOBILE UNIT EIGHT, in the town of Sigonella, Sicily, Italy. My dream was being realized on all fronts. Here I was assigned to a forward-deployed EOD Mobile Unit in the homeland of my grandparents. Josephine and Dominick Pizzini emigrated from Ascoli Piceno, Italy, to the Chicago Illinois, via Argentina, in 1943. From 1993-1996 my team deployed throughout Eastern and Western Europe, the Middle east and Western Asia, diving to locate and neutralize explosives from distant and not-so-distant conflicts. My small team of EOD operators and our equipment were considered lightweight and highly portable, so we went everywhere, and did everything a small team of EOD techs was expected to do—and then some.

My EOD teammates were awesome. The eight of us were assigned to a Mine Countermeasures (MCM) detachment (EODMU EIGHT DET FOUR). We dove the waters of the Mediterranean and Adriatic Seas, the Danish Eastern shore of Jutland in the Kattegat Sea near Åarhus, 116 miles northwest of Copenhagen, the North Sea and the inland waterways of The Netherlands, the Dardanelle Straights in Turkey at the entrance to the Sea of Marmara, and the Baltic Sea ports of Tallinn, Estonia, and Riga, Latvia, just to name a few. Using metal detectors we searched the battlefields of World War One in Eceabat, and Canaklale, Turkey. I was assigned to the Presidential Protection Detail for then President Clinton when he visited Belfast, Northern Ireland, Kiev, Ukraine, Minsk, Belarus, Naples, Italy, and Brussels, Belgium. I protected the First lady of the United States and Vice President Gore in Israel.

Life on and off duty was great. I had a three-bedroom villa overlooking the Gulf of Catania, and just beyond the gulf my view included Mount Etna, as it rose high above the city of Catania. Mount Etna is an active volcano and in addition to skiing on the volcano, we would watch it erupt from time to time. Being a tourist throughout Italy and beyond was awesome. We visited Vatican City, Pisa and the Leaning Tower, the canals of Venice, and the Colosseum of Rome. Sicily is also where I met my wife, Julie. She was on active duty and worked at the US Naval Hospital when we met. Many of my teammates returned to America with Italian wives, and I returned with an American girl from Colorado.

During this time, I was exposed to the highly capable leadership within Navy EOD, and I wanted greater responsibility. I was also selected for the rank of Chief Petty Officer, which is a significant promotion and an acceptance of much greater responsibility. It demonstrates a commitment to being a leader that not only meets, but exceeds, the expectations of the chain of command.

It was at this critical time in my career that I transferred to the Navy's premier diver training center in Panama City FL. I went from performing missions such as presidential protection, theatre exercises, mine recovery, locating and disabling explosives of all types on land and at sea, to leading a cadre of instructors in training the next generation of Navy EOD technicians. Instructor duty was something I knew I wanted to do ever since I was a student at 2C diver training in Pearl Harbor Hawaii, and 1C diver training in Panama City Florida in 1987. I recall the tough-as-nails instructors that shaped and molded me as a young Navy Diver, and I wanted to pay it forward at some point in my career.

Hard Learned Leadership Lessons

In 1998, two years into my tour as an instructor at the US Navy diving school, officially known as the Naval Diving and Salvage Training Center (NDSTC), Panama City Beach FL, I was summoned to the Commanding Officer's office. While I knew I would walk into his office on my own, I was fairly certain that I would leave his office in wrist shackles with military police escorting me to the brig.

Three days earlier I was the Diving Supervisor in charge of a diving operation in the Gulf of Mexico. My instructor cadre consisted of myself and four other Navy EOD technicians who lead the diving evolutions under my charge. On this day, we deployed from the NDSTC pier in our nine-meter rigid hulled inflatable boat (RHIB), a tactical marine vessel. With its twin Mercury Verado 250 hp 4-stroke outboard gasoline engines, this was a fun boat to operate. The mission was to conduct a final deep-water qualification dive for about 30 Navy diving students who were within days of graduation from this rigorous, high-risk training.

It was somewhat routine to bring our spear guns with us on these diving operations as there was dive site preparation that required our team of instructors to survey and assess the conditions which included placing a descent line and buoy in a strategically known location on the dive target, which was a shipwreck, for this operation.

During this initial diving evolution to set up, we would look for fish to spear with the hopes of putting amberjack, red snapper, or grouper on the dinner table. Spear fishing while conducting navy diving operations had always been controversial. Most leaders allowed it while others did not as this could distract from the purpose of the diving evolution. I personally enjoyed the sport so much that I did it recreationally, as did many other Navy Divers. Just before we pushed away from the pier, a coworker approached our boat and informed me that the Commanding Officer had ordered that there will be no more spear fishing while conducting Navy diving operations at NDSTC. I looked at my instructor cadre amongst the ice-filled coolers and spear guns on the tactical boat and said "this will be the last day that we spear fish during Navy diving operations."

The second Navy vessel for the day's diving operations was a 132-foot Yard Diving Tender (YDT). During these evolutions, the YDT transports the students, additional staff, and the crew to the dive site. During the diving prebrief, I instructed the craft master of the YDT on how to approach the dive site and told him to deploy a two-point moor which is the deployment of two anchors, one from the bow, and one from the stern, holding the vessel in place without the movement of a swing circle which occurs when a vessel uses a single bow anchor.

As the YDT approached the dive site, where my tactical boat and a civilian fishing boat were anchored, the wind and current began to interfere with the craft master's ability to maneuver. Having already released the stern anchor, the vessel was somewhat encumbered, which is normal during this anchoring procedure, however the wind and current proved to be too much for the craft master to successfully navigate. It became obvious to my boat crew and the civilian fishing vessel that this 132-foot craft was about to drift into us, slowly, but with certainly, and that this would cause damage to our boats and injury to all aboard.

To further complicate the situation, I had divers in the water. They were near the end of the prescribed bottom time and were due to reach the surface any second, just as this YDT was drifting into our boat and directly over the buoy where my divers were due to surface. The propellers on the YDT were turning at full power in an effort to avoid an at-sea collision. The propellers of on the YDT were directly over where my divers were due to surface.

Thankfully, and not surprisingly, my divers sensed the commotion and did not surface as planned. We managed the decompression profile while the YDT finally cleared the diving site. The civilian vessel released his anchor just before the YDT collided with him, and with great anger he headed to the pier of NDSTC. My boat was able to maneuver around the YDT avoiding misfortune. With all divers recovered onboard my tactical craft, we terminated the planned student qualification dives in order to return to the base and debrief this near miss, a term the Navy uses when things do not go according to plan and personal injury or equipment damage could have resulted.

When we returned to NDSTC, the Training Officer, my immediate boss, was waiting at the pier. The questioning immediately centered around spear fishing. "Were you spearfishing?" he asked. In my prepared response, I indicated that the spear guns had nothing to do with improper navigation of the YDT. After a brief discussion, I was directed to not report for duty for three days...a most unnerving three days. During the three days, the Training Officer investigated the incident, and reported his findings to the Commanding Officer. Some advisors to the Commanding Officer wanted him to throw the book at me while others recommended a lesser level of punishment.

These three days were spent with difficulty. I looked at myself in the mirror and realized how significantly I had failed. I failed all those above me in the chain of command, and all those who were under my charge. My status as one of the most respected leaders was in jeopardy, and it was one hundred percent my fault. During this time, my Commanding Officer had also been investigating, and considering what course of action to take with respect to my actions. He and I were quite familiar—we trained in the dive school gym at 0500, before anyone else. We traded martial arts techniques and spotted each other on the bench press. But now, he did not want to see me in the halls of his command. For three days I contemplated my poor decision-making and failure as a leader. For three days my Commanding Officer contemplated his decision as to my future in the US Navy.

When I finally entered his office, he motioned for me to sit down on the couch across from his large desk. He looked me squarely in the eye and asked, "Why is my number-one ranked chief sitting in front of me for violating a direct order? Did you get the order? Did you understand the order? Was something not clear?" As he offered me these outs, I felt the lump in my throat and the knot in my stomach develop. I could only be 100% honest.

> *"No sir, I understood the order" I said. I failed you and I failed my team, and I apologize professionally and personally and accept any action you deem necessary."*

My career could have taken a hard hit that day, due to my poor leadership. But, due to the great leadership of my Commanding Officer, he chose to give me a path to recovery. He stripped me of my leadership and technical qualifications to lead mixed-gas, deep sea diving operations, but he allowed me to repeat the apprenticeship process and regain my qualifications. I had to supervise operations under the instruction of people I had previously qualified and supervised. With no ego and no hesitation, I ran at one thousand mph to regain my qualifications. My pattern of working hard and mastering my craft emerged, as I truly loved my job and my teammates, and regained my status as an unlimited diving supervisor in short order. At the end of my instructor tour, after fifteen years in the enlisted ranks, I was selected for commissioning as a Naval Officer.

Why the long story? What did I learn? There are three big take-aways that every leader should take to heart.

1. You owe your leader 100% and nothing less. There is no 75% or 90% support of your leader. Give him or her 100% or go work somewhere else.

2. If you are a leader, you must require 100% from your team. If you accept less, the trend will spiral downward.

3. When a teammate comes up short...less than 100%, if they own the mistake, give them a path to recovery.

As terrible as I felt during that experience, I am better because of it. This is entirely due to my Commanding Officer having the foresight to be bold in his leadership. Some may call this a second chance. Most people I know have been on the receiving end of a second change. As leaders, we have to consider this second chance concept for those we lead.

Everyone has a previous life with errors and misfortunes that have helped define who you are today. It would be a mistake to disown these experiences because they are part of what makes you relatable to other humans, including your leadership team and employees. In a study of young adult males in the military, risky decision-making and reward sensitivity was more common when they were in a group of three same-age peers than when they were alone. In addition, having a slightly older adult present significantly reduces the risk of making poor decisions. The study also found that the social pressures of a peer group exert the same influence on decision-making and the attractiveness of an immediate reward as being mentally fatigued. It lowers your resolve to do the right thing.

Looking back on this experience, I can appreciate that the social context of my decision-making at the time might have been more influential than I realized. This gets to the value of operating within a team of trusted individuals, and the importance of having a variety of personalities and capabilities on your team. And speaking of my team, I felt terribly about letting them down, but as I reflected on what motivated me to make the decisions I made, and how my CO responded, a few things became more clear through the lens of time.

Forgiven vs Fired

Why do some people get another chance after making a significant error, while others get fired? Why didn't I get fired after violating the trust and confidence of my Commanding Officer? As I shared my defining moment with a friend and US Army Special Operator, he provided me with the following photo from his leadership notebook.

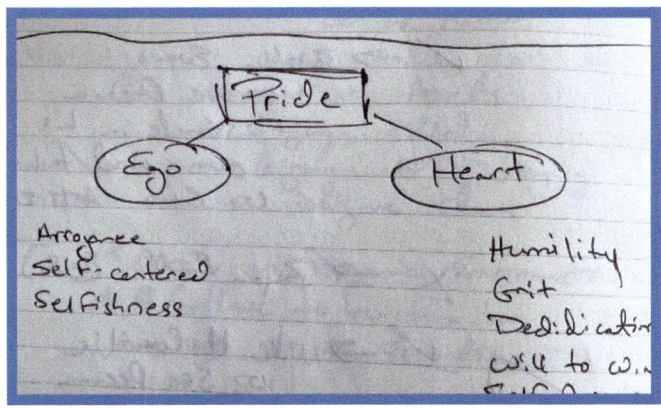

Everyone in military Special Operations has huge pride, huge egos, and huge hearts. Pride guides us to do good things on and off of duty. If you lead with heart, you can see from the picture that the dominant traits are humility, grit, dedication, and self-awareness, just to name a few. If you lead primarily with ego, the traits of arrogance, self-centeredness or self-interest, and selfishness are dominant. If you have established a reputation that is ego-driven, you are more likely to be relieved of your responsibilities after making a significant mistake. If, however, you are known to lead with your heart, odds are that you will be put on a path to recovery. This has been my experience and observation throughout my military career, and it is true in the private sector. As I look back on the few people that I fired over the past 10 years, most had their egos, or their loyalty, misaligned.

Fast forward to 2002, when I was the Operations Officer at Explosive Ordnance Disposal (EOD) MOBILE UNIT FIVE in Guam. I was responsible for nine operationally assigned EOD detachments, each consisting of six to eight personnel. I would deploy these EOD teams to aircraft carriers, amphibious ships, the jungles of The Republic of the Philippines and Thailand, and even Viet Nam and North Korea on Prisoner of War (POW) and Missing In Action (MIA) recovery missions in support of The Joint POW/MIA Accounting Command, a task force within the United States Department of Defense (DoD) whose mission is to account for Americans who are listed as Prisoners of War, or Missing in Action, from all past wars and conflicts. Within my Operations Department I had five people who reported directly to me. One of these five, a Chief who was a good EOD Technician and a good person, was nearing the end of his active-duty career, and going through a separation that led to divorce. His performance had notably declined.

Upon completion of a major exercise in and around Thailand in 2002, I gathered all EODMU FIVE personnel to debrief the weeks-long exercise which included complex diving operations, static line and military freefall parachute operations, counter terrorist/counter improvised Explosive Devise (IED) operations, and command and control with our headquarters overseeing operations from Guam. In my remarks during the debrief I recognized those who I thought went above and beyond the call of duty. I said that some on our team do what they do because they love doing it, some do it for recognition, and some are along for the ride (I probably could have spoken more eloquently, but I was speaking my mind). In April of 2021, nineteen years after this exercise in Thailand, the chief that I mentioned above, who was on that exercise in Thailand, visited me at my business in Virginia Beach. He recounted the story above, and said it was at that moment, during my debrief in Thailand, that he took a hard look at his life and refocused on the remainder of his active-duty career, and success in the civilian sector. He completed his active-duty career with distinction and continues to enjoy great success in the private sector. I was not trying to change anybody's life that day, (or maybe I was) but the fact that he considers that to be a defining moment in his life is something I have to embrace and appreciate. Just as I remember each word that was spoken with my Commanding Officer in Panama City Florida, the EOD Chief remembers my words from nineteen years ago in a land far, far away. That was one of his defining moments, and I am honored to have helped him.

DRILL: Reflect on one or more defining moments that shaped your leadership experience, capture the lifelong lessons learned, and develop a story to tell yourself and others about that experience.

CHAPTER 3: CONSTRUCTING YOUR LEADERSHIP FOUNDATION

BLUF: Solid Leadership requires a good foundation

In 1995, I visited the Leaning Tower of Pisa when I was stationed in Italy. It was great fun as we rode our Harley Davidson motorcycles from Sicily to Silkeborg, Denmark.

The Leaning Tower of Pisa (Italian: torre pendente di Pisa) or simply the Tower of Pisa (torre di Pisa ['torre di 'pi:za; 'pi:sa][1]) is the campanile, or freestanding bell tower, of the cathedral of the Italian city of Pisa, known worldwide for its nearly 5.5-degree lean, the result of an unstable foundation, which was discovered at the time of construction.

As I mentioned in the preface, great leaders have a solid foundation which they have carefully constructed over time. Unless leaders construct—and continue to care for—that foundation they risk looking up one day to find a 5.5° lean creating instability. The main purpose of a foundation is to hold the structure above it and keep it upright. A poorly constructed building foundation can be dangerous to the occupants and the neighborhood. A leader's foundation must support the immediate team, the business operation, and stakeholder expectations. Just as a highly visible skyscraper needs a secure foundation, today's highly visible executive also needs a foundation that is deep, wide, and largely unseen, to survive the onslaught of attack, and risk, from both internal and external sources. While defending against these attacks, such as a pandemic and societal lockdown, modern leaders must also be perceptive enough to recognize and create opportunities for the business and the team to flourish.

You probably possess the innate skills and instincts necessary to be the kind of person others naturally think of as a leader. But do you think and feel that way about yourself? There are at least three dozen leadership "styles" described in various books and writings on the topic. You will come away from this chapter and the overall experience delving into the art and science of leadership with a better mental model of your leadership definition, styles and power types, and which to apply in various situations. You will also be energized and inspired to continue honing your leadership definition, and overall brand of leadership over time and with experience.

As we begin this process of deliberately developing and reinforcing your foundation, think about the needs of your company and your team as they live through the current pandemic or other challenges. Your leadership foundation should provide you with secure footing during dynamic times as you feel the shift beneath your feet. This investment in a solid foundation, crafted in a manner that will literally last for the remainder of your life, will afford you the ability to be a great leader of many people for a very long time. For those who already have a trusted foundation, this exercise and those that follow will provide an opportunity to reexamine and reinforce your foundation, adapting it and strengthening it to withstand the challenges of today and the demands placed on the modern leader.

Your foundation has three main components.

- Your personal definition of leadership
- Deliberate leadership styles
- Deliberate power types

Your Personal Definition of Leadership

As we dive into the art of leadership, let's begin this construction project by examining the definition of the word "art" as defined by Merriam-Webster.

Art

: skill acquired by experience, study, or observation

the art of making friends

Skill acquired by experience, study, or observation. Does this sound like a significant component of leadership? My three pillars for great leadership are **experience, education, and training**. Human creative skill is the essence of art, whether it be in a visual form, musical form, physical form such as sports or the performing arts, and certainly in our daily activities as we lead ourselves and others. Remember, we want to build a foundation that is both deep and wide.

Now let's take a look at a few definitions and observations regarding the word leadership.

"Leadership is the knack of getting somebody to do something you want done because he wants to do it" — General Dwight D. Eisenhower

"Leadership and learning are indispensable to each other" – JFK

Warren Bennis said, "leadership is the capacity to translate vision into reality."

The Air Force defines leadership as "the art and science of influencing and directing people to accomplish the assigned mission."

Oxford Dictionary lead·er·ship /ˈlēdərˌSHip/ noun, The action of leading a group of people or an organization.

"The single biggest way to impact an organization is to focus on leadership development." – John Maxwell

"Leadership is enabling others to achieve their objectives, and requires comprehensive awareness, developed through experience, education, and training." – Robert Pizzini

The USAF definition includes the words art and science. There are books written about the art and science of leadership, including this one, however, my discussion and definitions for the art and science of leadership are significantly different than anything you have been exposed to in the past. Typical university-level discussions regarding the "science of leadership" tend to have a more nerdy, analytical approach. It is often linear, mission-oriented, and describes leading based on observations and metrics only.

The entire second half of this book is dedicated to the science of leadership as defined by me, and is a 100% departure from any previous discussion regarding the science of leadership. How is my approach different? I believe the science of leadership is driven by your attention to physiology—your physical and mental health. But for now, back to the art of leadership.

At this point you should begin formulating your own definition of leadership. Some leadership organizations recommend that you develop a personal mission statement. My observation is that this is the same as developing your own definition of the word leadership. If you develop and adhere to your own personal definition of leadership, you will know when you are leading, and when you are not leading. I can break my definition down to two words...Enabling Others. John Maxwell does it even better with the one-word definition, Influence. As you can see in my full definition above, I believe that leadership is "enabling others to achieve their objectives." Those objectives can be for the good of the workplace and ROI, professional and personal development, or other interests. I further believe that every highly capable leader has gone through the crucible of formal education, years of experience (Gladwell's 10,000 hours comes to mind), and has attended hundreds of micro training events up to the point of becoming an influential and memorable leader.

The last page of this chapter provides a template for you to begin to develop your own definition of leadership. Turn to that page throughout this chapter to capture your personal thoughts on leadership. You can simply adapt to an existing definition that suits your brand, or you can develop your own definition. My definition has evolved over time, to include minor changes as recently as a few months ago.

Now that you have a personal definition of leadership, you have the cornerstone of your foundation in place.

The Three Pillars

In my personal definition of leadership, I mentioned the three pillars of **experience**, **education**, and **training**. Let's take a moment to break down these pillars, beginning with experience.

Experience: Leadership experience often occurs early in one's life. You may have held leadership positions on your sports team, scouts, school clubs such as debate and band, or perhaps babysitting. These childhood experiences are the seeds of leadership. As you planted these seeds, your experience as a leader began to take shape and even grew. You probably adopted a style of leadership that resembled your parents, teachers, and coaches. This was also probably unconscious leadership in that perhaps you did not view yourself as a leader.

Let's shift to experience in the workplace. If you are responsible for anyone other than yourself, you are in a leadership position. In my consulting work I often encounter small- to mid-sized businesses that do not pay attention to leadership development until there is an issue. In a typical small business, the entrepreneur is focused on the product or service and leadership development is not on the radar. Fast forward a few years, after the company has grown and hired additional staff: these new hires are likely to be proficient at the skill set you hired them to perform, but they also need to be led. Processes, programs, and budgets are among the things that are managed, but people need to be led. More on this in Chapter 5, where I discuss the age-old dichotomy of leadership vs. management.

Your team needs to see a strong leader who can communicate the corporate vision. This is also a time when mistakes are made as leadership is not given its due. All of us, myself included, have made mistakes that we regret in leading our teams. We have also made great decisions that resulted in success. These early experiences in leadership should be captured in the conscious mind to build upon. Take a moment here to reflect on your early experiences as a leader which will help you be empathetic in developing those you currently lead, or those who you will be leading soon.

Education: Formal education is a key component of leadership in my experience. Education gives you, the leader, tools in decision making, whether or not you recognize this aspect of your leadership. Education develops, among other things, your ability to communicate across the various communication channels—internal, external, horizontal, vertical, written, spoken, and many others. Reading this book falls under both education and training. I also firmly believe that education alone is not nearly enough to prepare someone for a leadership role. As Joe Despenza wrote in his book *Breaking the Habit of Being Yourself*, "education without experience is merely philosophy." Education has many forms, from university level instruction to professional development, to investing the time in reading a book like this. I believe that a balance of formal education along with other educational experiences enable the best leader within you to emerge.

When I enlisted in the Navy in 1984, I had no desire to go to college. I couldn't even spell the word. Thanks to engaged leaders, and the military's tuition assistance program, I began to take college courses here and there. After 12 years of active duty and an evaluation of all my military schooling by the American College of Education (ACE) up to that point, I needed only four specific classes to complete a bachelor's degree. How did that happen? I still remember where I was and the gentleman who worked at Navy College in Pensacola FL who informed me that I was close to a bachelor's degree. By now I had developed a desire to further my education. Having travelled the world up to this point and witnessed both the great accomplishments and tragedies of humanity, I developed an interest in international relations, national security, and terrorism, which was the course of study for my graduate degree. Again, the military's tuition assistance program was too valuable not to use. In obtaining a graduate degree, I learned as much or more about how to research and write as I did about international relations, national security, and counterterrorism. I never imagined that this experience would lead to the writing of this book.

Training: Micro training events throughout one's career are critical to leadership development. Training topics are various and can include almost anything. Email etiquette for example is one such micro training event. Email is considered official business communication. What does this have to do with leadership? As the leader of an organization, department, or simply leading others on a team, you will be well served to require those you lead to use proper email etiquette. Email can easily be forwarded for the world to see. Ultimately, the author of an email represents the organization, which reflects upon the leadership within that organization. Other micro training events that I have attended over the years include communication, decision making, team-building to include forming, storming, norming, and performing, just to name a few. My one-day seminar, two day off-site, and three-day retreat are leadership training events. Franklin Covey, Dale Carnegie, John Maxwell, and various other training organizations offer hundreds of micro training events and topics. Deep dives on these various topics are a great way to develop your subordinates if you have them research the material and present their takeaways to your team. In my weekly staff meeting with my leadership team, we review aspects of leadership through book reviews and other micro training events.

Throughout my military experience, most training events had three components, and these three components apply to everything from aviation, to commanding a US Navy warship, to defusing bombs, to leading others. The first component is the **classroom**, where theory and technical aspects are presented. This often requires rote memorization and an understanding of new concepts. Knowledge retention is often tested via written or oral exams.

The second component is in a **lab** setting. The lab allows the trainee to take the theory of the classroom and apply it, under controlled conditions, often using a checklist or other form of supervision. The lab is designed to allow for mistakes, often repeating the various steps in a process. One variation of a lab setting is called a tabletop exercise, or TTX. A TTX is usually discussion-based, where a scenario is presented and the participants talk through the various steps that lead to the desired outcome. With the theory of the classroom, and the practical application of the lab behind us, we move on to the third component, a field exercise.

A field exercise (**fieldex**) is the application of the newly acquired skill set in real world conditions. This can range from diving to the depths of the world's oceans, to leading a platoon of special operators to search for, locate, identify, and dispose of terrorist explosive devices, to integrating your team with other operational elements. The fieldex is a great place to fail. This is where developing leaders will make decisions, right or wrong, usually with great confidence. Often, you are expected to fail. The fieldex may have been designed with a no-win scenario. FUBAR comes to mind. In these moments, you are expected to act, to lead, regardless of the dire setting. The learning that occurs in a fieldex is what separates military leadership development from that of the commercial world. Rather than be fired or otherwise replaced, failure to some degree is tolerated because we don't walk alone in the military. We own our shortcomings and live to fight another day. Replacing a trained warrior is not easy, nor is replacing a highly trained teammate in most professions.

Deliberate Leadership Styles

We will now add bricks to your foundation, and those bricks consist of leadership styles and power types. The research and literature on these two topics is well beyond the scope of this book, however, I have addressed the most common leadership styles in a podcast entitled "The Art of Leadership - Elevate Your Leadership." An Internet search will produce numerous treatises regarding the 6-best, or the 9-best, or the 12-best leadership styles. Which styles suit your personal brand, preferences, and overall approach? Let's begin with a close look at a few leadership styles to get you acclimated to the concept.

A cursory Google search will reveal the following leadership styles amongst the most common:

Autocratic Style, Authoritative Style, Pacesetting Style, Democratic Style, Coaching Style, Affiliative Style, and Laissez-Faire Style.

You may note that I did not list Servant Leadership as a style, although there is much written and taught regarding servant leadership. For me, being a servant leader is an ever-present critical trait of a leader, and I will address my 10 critical traits of a leader in the next chapter.

We will break down visionary, coaching, and participative, my top three preferred styles, including some pros and cons, to set you in motion. We will also briefly discuss the directive style of leadership. In this discussion, I am encouraging you to review and adopt several leadership styles, while keeping others in mind depending on the situation. In addition, I believe that you should define each style in your own terms as I have done below. Remember, leadership is a personal brand and the more you can personalize your brand of leadership, the better. Once again, the last page of this chapter is designed for you to capture your preferred leadership styles.

Visionary Leadership Style

Visionary leadership is highly successful and a requirement in any organization. A visionary leader sets the cardinal direction (a phrase from Marty Strong's book *Be Nimble*), a long-term vision that is constantly reinforced by the leader. This vision defines the strategy and ultimately execution. Leaders must be clear about the long-term goals and develop each member of the team to pursue the vision resulting in successful business operations and outcomes. Successful visionary leaders create productive businesses that make employees feel they are directly contributing to the success of the company. There are no cons to a visionary style of leadership other than to not have a clearly crafted vision for your organization.

Coaching Leadership Style

This style is generally accepted as a very positive aspect of the workplace. Leaders who adopt the coach style invest in each individual and take the time to build individual skills for success. When an experienced leader applies the coaching style, the leader brings out what is already within the individual. As a USA Hockey Level 5 coach (more leadership training) I apply some of the principles of coaching on the ice to coaching within my business. One aspect of coaching is reviewing past activity and asking your employee (or hockey player) if faced with a similar situation in the future, would you do anything different…and what would that be? This could be followed by a brief walk-through, or rehearsal. I will address the importance of rehearsals in the critical traits discussion in the next chapter. The pros of the coach style include great employee engagement and a sense of belonging on the team, while a con would be that professional boundaries could break down a bit. For example, anytime the boss is spending time one-on-one with employees, others may question this activity. Be a good coach, and coach every player on your team. In ice hockey as we strive to be good coaches, we often remind ourselves to not be a kid's last coach.

Participative Leadership Style

I am a big proponent of participative leadership but this is often referred to as a democratic or shared leadership. In my experience, participative leadership can offer value, and is distinctly different than a democratic style. Participative leaders usually ask for team member input. Your customer-facing teammates, those who deliver the product or service usually have a good grasp of the ground truth. Therefore, a smart leader invites them to participate in problem-solving and offering solutions. Democratic leaders, on the other hand, allow for input in every decision and bring all matters for a vote. Voting is good for deciding on whether we get a ping pong table or a pool table in the break room but not for major decisions such budgets, investment in renovation or training, etc. This can be quite disruptive and limit the power and influence of the leader. We will dive deeper into this in Chapter 5 when we explore voice vs vote.

Directive Leadership Style (aka Authoritative)

Although the directive style is not one of my preferred styles, it is important to know what it means to be directive so you can avoid it, or use it when necessary. Directive leaders may communicate a "my way or the highway" methodology which is purely authoritative and destructive to say the least. When teammates operate with the constant fear of screwing up or losing their job, they tire and will leave. Whether it is a sales goal or a customer service process, this style also inhibits the formation of a positive culture, which is critical to sustained operations with highly engaged employees. We discussed culture in Chapter 1 as the factor that matters most in the workplace, and we will revisit the components of good culture in Chapter 5. On the other hand, there is a time and place for the directive style. Military operations, police, fire, and EMS all have a directive nature when dealing with emergencies and extreme situations. These extreme situations can also occur in any workplace. Therefore, although directive is not one of my preferred styles, I will use it if the situation warrants.

12 additional styles include:

Servant

Autocratic

Laissez-faire or hands-off

Transformational

Transactional

Bureaucratic

Authoritarian

Participative

Delegative

Situational

Pace Setter

Charismatic

And there are more.

Now that you have a basic understanding of leadership styles, let's take it to the next level through a practical exercise—a self-assessment. You may have a sense of your leadership styles already, or at least a sense of what you would like to convey when you interact with others in your organization. In other words, how do you want to be perceived?

Do you remember the great leaders that you worked for? How about the not-so-great ones? What about your teachers and coaches? Many people in leadership positions have a style that they largely inherited from early experiences rather than consciously developing their own style. Their words and actions are largely the words and actions of previous leaders such as parents, coaches, teachers, and employers. This leads us to consciousness and the art of modern leadership.

Take a moment for the following reflection, and make a few notes on page 73-74 to record the positive and negative attributes which come to mind:

> Take a moment to think about the leaders you admire, those who guided you during a formative moment of your life as a child, young adult, and as a developing professional.
>
> Now think about those who impeded your progress and caused you to think about moving in a different direction, either away from that team, that school, that department, or organization.

These two reflections will guide you through developing your preferred leadership styles. Using the checklist on page 73-74, make a list of the positive attributes of leaders that you admire. Then make a list of the negative attributes that you have experienced. I'm not talking about a list of "ideal" attributes. I want you to picture in your mind the people that you remember for better or worse when it comes to leadership. Capture the positive attributes and revisit them often, daily perhaps. Same for the negative attributes, review them regularly and be sure that you do not display them in your day-to-day activities. You are now consciously developing your personal brand as a leader. Ultimately, you will identify definitive leadership styles that you refer to weekly, if not daily.

My top three preferred styles of leadership are visionary, coach, and participative. Although the "directive" style is not one that I prefer to use, I will be directive if the situation requires this style. However, if I apply my three preferred styles correctly, the need to be directive is unlikely to present itself.

Deliberate Power Types

We will now add even more bricks to your foundation: types of power. Leaders use power to accomplish their objectives. Power is largely based on your reputation and credibility, and can be wielded properly, abused, and even ignored. Leaders must be well trained to cultivate power and use it with tact. In short, when people perceive you in a power position, they are relying on you and there's a lot you can achieve through influence. If you Google power types just as you did with leadership styles, once again you will find treatises regarding the 5-best or the 9-best or the 12 best power types, and just as with leadership styles, power types are largely adaptable to your personality traits and leadership brand. Let's closely examine four power types:

Legitimate Power

This power exists in a clearly defined hierarchical model. The higher up in the model, the more legitimate power one has over others. Legitimate power is usually assigned or given, depending on the specific requirements of a particular position. Everyone in the organization recognizes the legitimate power this person has, and follows directives appropriately. Legitimate power can also be taken away if not managed properly, or if the appointment was temporary, for a specific project perhaps. I will even go so far as to say that legitimate power is lost if those under you lose respect for you. Ultimately, those you lead must have confidence in your ability to lead. If confidence is lost, it is difficult to effectively lead.

Referent Power

This power is developed over time and results in high levels of trust and respect, while cultivating meaningful relationships inside and outside of the organization. For me, this is the most important power one can develop and put to use. Referent power is the type of power that enables you to pursue bold initiatives because all on the team believe strongly in you as their leader. Referent power takes time to establish, however, it can be lost quickly if trust is compromised.

Connection Power

Do you know any connectors? Connection power is developed by building networks inside and outside of your organization. Not to be confused with informational power, connection power can be activated when you deliver the right information to the right people. Politicians use the power of connection in their daily activities. Connection power can be temporary or indefinite depending on the frequency of interaction with others.

Coercive Power

This is simply leading by threatening. *Do this, or else*. I, rightly or wrongly, assume that people know the negative consequences of not performing properly in the workplace. This is a power type that has no real value. If you have to be coercive, there is likely a bigger issue to address. I have made the mistake of using this power type early in my career as it was used on me. As parents, we tend to use this power type in the interest of the well-being of our children, but I do not like to be coercive under any circumstance.

A other few common power types include:

- Informational power – having information that another does not have, and distributing that information as a means of bringing about change.
- Expert power – an individual uses knowledge or expertise in an area that they are responsible for to influence others.

The application of power types is the same as leadership styles. You must first define each style, be aware of the pros and cons, and apply the appropriate power type to each situation. This is best achieved when these power types reside in the conscious mind. It takes years of conscious leadership to develop "muscle memory" in applying leadership styles and power types, as with other activities such as sports or martial arts.

The Art

Recall the definition of art: a skill acquired by experience, study, or observation.

This chapter has guided you through considering your own experiences, study, and observation of other leaders. Your challenge before moving on is to develop your personal definition of leadership and a sense of your preferred leadership styles and power types. Just as an artist blends the colors on his or her palette to get the sought-after hue, so, too, does a leader blend the foundational elements presented here to achieve the desired outcome for any given situation. You have some flexibility in drawing from these deliberate leadership styles and power types in crafting your brand of leadership. Regardless of your unique brand, all leaders are characterized by a set of specific leadership traits. In the next chapter I will present the ten leadership traits that I consider to be the most critical.

DRILL:
1. Complete your personal leadership profile on the next page.
2. Recognize opportunities to consciously apply these principles of leadership, then be metacognitive of the results, and document the experience in your leader's logbook.

PERSONAL LEADERSHIP PROFILE

(This page should be designed to look like an artist's palette):

Draft your definition of leadership

_____
_____
_____

If you're stuck, try this:

Leadership is … _____

choose from one of the following: enabling/influencing/engaging/empowering/facilitating/inspiring/

and one of the following: employees/teachers/students/medical professionals/nurses/doctors/engineers/sales professionals/others

to _____.
              (do what?)

Leadership Styles – choose three which seem best suited to your definition of leadership

- ☐ Visionary
- ☐ Coaching
- ☐ Participative
- ☐ Directive
- ☐ Servant
- ☐ Autocratic
- ☐ Laissez-faire or hands-off
- ☐ Transformational

- ☐ Transactional
- ☐ Bureaucratic
- ☐ Authoritarian
- ☐ Participative
- ☐ Delegative
- ☐ Situational
- ☐ Pace Setter
- ☐ Charismatic

Power Types – choose three which seem best suited to your definition of leadership

- ☐ Legitimate
- ☐ Referent
- ☐ Connection
- ☐ Coercive
- ☐ Reward
- ☐ Informational
- ☐ Expert

Three Pillars

What have you done this year to support your Three Pillars? Do you have plans to participate in any experience, education or training this year?

- Experience   -
  _____

- Education   -
  _____

- Training   -
  _____

CHAPTER 4: ELEVEN CRITICAL TRAITS

BLUF: Have specific "go to" tactics and techniques and look for opportunities to deploy them

Now that you have all the building blocks in place with your personal definition of leadership, your preferred leadership styles, and your preferred power types, the following ten critical traits of leadership will serve as the mortar that creates a solid bond which extends throughout and beyond your foundation. While many leaders have certain principles that they believe in, I have come to rely on ten specific traits that I consider to be critical to steady, sound leadership. You may identify different critical traits than the list that follows. I also evolve this critical trait list from time to time. Very few things in leadership are completely static. I used to live by my nine critical traits, but decided to add a tenth. With these ten critical traits in the conscious mind, they are easy to reflect upon given the situation you find yourself in. Let's get straight to it.

1. **Student leader**

You may have heard the example of a 10th degree black belt who shows up at the dojo wearing a white belt and says to all the students: "somebody teach me something." Regardless of how long you have been in your craft, there is more to learn. Often, we think we know more about our craft than newcomers, or those with less time in the business than we have. I deliberately give those who work for me the opportunity to teach me something, even if it is something that I already know, because often I need a review or a refresher, or there have been revisions to the process. Being a student for those under your charge also gives your teammates a chance to showcase their knowledge or skill. In the military we call this a dog and pony show. The Admiral or General shows up to have a look at the command or a unit within the command, and the team presents their capabilities and equipment, often with some type of demonstration. This was particularly fun for us, as explosives were our primary tools. The Admiral or General has seen this dog and pony show many times, but it gives the tactical level troops an opportunity to engage the highest levels of leadership within the US military, and it is empowering for the troops, which contributes significantly to a positive culture.

For me, being a student leader is different than being a student *of* leadership, although there are similarities such as learning in general. Being a student of leadership is similar to the practice of yoga, or any other practice where you deliberately and continuously try to improve upon the practice. Being a student, for me, is usually quite enjoyable.

2. Flex and Adapt

"Flexibility in our lives means having a fundamental ability to relate to any new environment and excel in it. Instead of fighting it, you greet it with open arms and observe it; instead of criticizing it, you caress it and understand it; instead of ignoring it, you make it yours and be one with it."— Sun Tzu, The Art of War.

Charles Darwin can be quoted in stating ... "It's not the strongest of species that survives, nor the most intelligent, but the one most responsive to change."

The verb form of flex means to bend. The verb form of adapt means to make suitable; to correspond; to fit or suit; to adjust to new conditions. To adapt is to make changes that suit a condition or environment. In the military, especially regarding intelligence, we say that if the information is 20 minutes old, it is outdated and has changed. I believe this to be true in the private sector as well.

In 2001, when I was stationed in Guam I was the Officer In Charge (OIC) of a counterterrorism detachment and working to complete a graduate degree. As I studied International Relations, National

Security, Diplomacy, and Terrorism, I recall reading that nation states with flexibility and adaptability have a greater tendency to thrive, while very rigid countries experience greater levels of conflict and poverty. This resonated with me immediately as I observed that people who are the most flexible and adaptable are the most successful. We all flex and adapt as a course of our daily lives, but those who consciously remind themselves to flex and adapt are much better at it. Weather changes, seasons change, people change, and nothing stays the same. The more you remind yourself of this, the faster and more effectively you will flex and adapt.

Some may call this resilience, the ability to respond to and recover from adversity. In war, the side most able to modify the strategy in response to resource constraints, weather, or new intelligence is best able to gain the upper hand. When adversity strikes, flex and adapt. Ask yourself, "how can I flex and adapt to the current situation?" I have also heard this aspect of leadership compared to bamboo, one of the strongest materials to grow in nature, yet admired for its flexible qualities in enduring extreme conditions without failing. Bruce Lee famously said "notice that the stiffest tree is most easily cracked, while the bamboo or willow survives by bending in the wind."

3. Recognize Leadership Opportunities

I believe that this critical trail is often, and easily, overlooked. In the normal workday, one of your employees could do something seemingly mundane, but if they hadn't done the task, how far off course would the day have gone? How adversely could that have affected your organization? Do you acknowledge that their day-to-day commitment is vital to the success of the organization? That could be a water-cooler moment, a drive-by in the hallway, a quick social media post, etc. People appreciate being recognized for their efforts. It is easy for a leader to use these opportunities to make a connection, say thank you, and recognize leadership at the team level.

Another example occurred recently. My 17-year-old son and I were driving on Interstate 95, just south of Washington DC, on our way to hockey camp, when a rear tire blew. What began as a bit of an imbalance ended with a loud pop as the tire detonated. Luckily, we were near an exit ramp and immediately got to a safe shoulder location. I grabbed my phone and began to call USAA emergency roadside service, when my son asked if we were going to change the tire. I put the phone down and said, "hell yes we are going to change the tire." Within minutes my son located the jack behind the backseat of my Ford F150 pick-up. We ensured that traffic conditions were safe to change out the tire in the 95-degree heat, then got to work. Within 30 minutes the spare tire was on and we were back on the road chugging water (much more on drinking water in Part II) and fist bumping our success. Although we worked together, I encouraged him to lead the effort, and tell me how I could help. All the while, I had my eye on safety, efficiency, and quality. If I was alone, I would have remained in the air-conditioned interior of my truck and called USAA roadside assistance.

Another example comes to mind. A young lady on my customer service team renovated and updated our standard operating procedures on her own initiative. She was also on her way to college at Virginia Tech. When I saw the great work she did, I asked her to put together an executive summary of her actions and present it to the leadership team. This task was less about informing the leadership team and more about giving this young lady the experience of presenting. Needless to say, she did a wonderful job.

Every organization I have been involved with seeks out volunteers to lead certain efforts. This could include organizing the company softball team, investigating an HR issue, redesigning office space, or reviewing the hiring process. Volunteering for these one-off assignments will give you informational authority and some level of autonomous leadership. More importantly, you will help build your leadership brand by volunteering for such efforts. Finally, by simply sharing your critical traits with those you lead through focused discussion you will strengthen your bond while developing leaders among your team.

4. Peak, Trough, Recovery

In a book titled *When*, written by Daniel Pink, the author discusses three states of energy and awareness that most of us (80% of adults) experience each day. The first state is peak. This is a state where you are highly analytical, focused, energized, and you can get the tough work done. You keep distractions at bay. For most of us, we enter a peak state shortly after awakening from a restful night's sleep, usually around 30-60 minutes after our feet hit the floor. Although we think coffee helps get us in a peak state, it's actually your body's release of the cortisol awakening response (CAR). You naturally experience what should be your largest daily release of cortisol during this period. Peak usually lasts several hours and will remain through early afternoon, aided by the body's natural release of serotonin. (We will talk more about hormone release in Chapter 7.)

As the peak state diminishes, it is then followed by the trough state. Trough is when your mental acuity is at a low point where you can't seem to focus or concentrate. It's tough to get anything done. Trough is enhanced by what you ate for breakfast, and what you eat for lunch. Eyes may become heavy in trough. Then, astonishingly, in the late afternoon hours we enter into the recovery state. Recovery is not the same high energy and activity that you experience during the peak state, and it's not the doldrum of a trough. Recovery is more related to activities associated with brain storming. Recovery is a bit of a second wind. Hopefully you remember my application of mono-stereo-surround sound from the Ground Rules. As we discuss peak, trough, and recovery, you want to be aware of what state you are in, as well as what state others are in. If I am requesting something from someone, it's best to make that request when the individual is in their peak state.

Daniel Pink's book gives several examples of how negotiation is much more successful when all concerned are in their peak. In Part II of this book we will explore how rest, hydration, nutrition, exercise, brain and heart health, and lifelong learning are critical to achieving and extending your peak state. With awareness of these conditions, I now put critical tasks during times of not only my peak, but the peak of my immediate team. If scheduling a negotiation, I try to time it with the high energy or peak state of the person I am negotiating with. Once again, 80% of the population experience peak in the morning hours. I have had success with scheduling important discussions and negotiations in the am hours. Equally important, I put the more mundane tasks in the trough time zone.

5. Metacognition

Thinking about thinking...Metacognition is just that. It is awareness and understanding of one's own thought processes and how those processes were developed. It is a trait that good leaders exercise often. Thinking about your cognitive process will give you better control of your cognitive processes. Do you take time each day to simply think? Do you have a thinking process? Thinking about how you think, then making deliberate improvements in how you think is a very powerful process. How do you know if you are doing it correctly? Simple. Did you find value in the process? If yes, you are effectively being metacognitive. Examples of metacognitive activities include planning how to approach a learning task, using appropriate skills and strategies to solve a problem, monitoring one's own comprehension of text, self-assessing and self-correcting in response to the self-assessment, and evaluating progress toward the completion of a task. How does this apply to leadership? Let us consider the Dunning-Kruger Effect.

The Dunning-Kruger effect is a phenomenon that describes how some people believe they're much smarter, more competent, or capable than they really are. In 1999, Cornell University social psychologist David Dunning and graduate student Justin Kruger coined the term in their article, "Unskilled and Unaware of It," in the *Journal of Personality and Social Psychology*. The article summarized the findings of their research, revealing that an alarming percentage of people who score in the lowest percentile of certain tests drastically overestimate their own performance. The study covers all aspects of life to include the workplace and leadership in politics, government, and the private sector. It cites among other negative traits, the lack of metacognition among incompetent or ineffective leaders. Being metacognitive means, among other things, that you—as a leader—think about your ability as a leader and how you can constantly become better. Since learning about metacognition in 2019, I spend 10 minutes or so each day simply thinking. I usually close my eyes, but not always. I may go for a walk and engage the metacognitive process. This ultimately provides moments of great clarity for me, and I am sure that you will realize the same benefit.

6. The 5-Why Challenge

The 5-Whys is an iterative interrogative technique used to explore the cause-and-effect relationships underlying a particular problem. The primary goal of the technique is to determine the root cause of a defect or problem by repeating the question "Why?" Each answer forms the basis of the next question. The "five" in the name derives from an anecdotal observation on the number of iterations needed to resolve the problem.

The 5-Whys process is part of the Toyota Production System. Developed by Sakichi Toyoda, a Japanese inventor and industrialist, the technique became an integral part of the Lean philosophy. Toyoda developed the 5 Whys technique in the 1930s. It became popular in the 1970s, and Toyota still uses it to solve problems today. With today's connectivity, there are many websites with various five why tools and methods to apply this fairly basic, but highly effective, system.

Not all problems have a single root cause. If one wishes to uncover multiple root causes, the method must be repeated asking a different sequence of questions each time.

The method provides no hard and fast rules about what lines of questions to explore, or how long to continue the search for additional root causes. Thus, even when the method is closely followed, the outcome still depends upon the knowledge and persistence of the people involved.

Let's use real-world COVID-era problem: congestion in the lobby of our ice rink which contributed to an outbreak.

Why #1: Why is there so much congestion in the lobby with our COVID protocols for distancing in place?

Because the parents are gathering in the lobby as the kids come off the ice.

Why #2: Why are the parents gathering in the lobby?

Because when the kids come off the ice they are stopping in the lobby.

Why #3: Why are the kids stopping in the lobby?

Because they are starting to take off their gear.

Why #4: Why are the kids starting to take off gear in the lobby when our COVID protocols direct that they do so outside?

Because they start with their skates, and out of habit start removing the rest of their equipment.

Why #5: Why are they removing the rest of their gear instead of walking out after taking skates off?

Because their gear bag is right under the bench in the lobby.

Root cause: The gear bag is in the building.

Solution: If we do not allow the bag in the building, kids will ungear outside and the parents will move out of the lobby immediately after practice. We also made sure to address the barriers to adopting this practice by talking to parents and coaches. In response to their suggestions, we created an outdoor locker room with lights, seating, and provided mats so kids could walk directly to these outdoor locker rooms with their skates still on. This provided a way to clear the rink quickly and allow kids to hang out, talk, and joke around without increasing the chances of spreading virus in a closed space.

A well known 5-Why example involves the work of Don Messersmith, whose study on the lighting of the memorials in Washington D. C. has become one of the best known teaching of the 5-Whys method. Because source documents are difficult to locate, many different versions of the tale exist today. And while you may have learned a slightly different version, the general details of the story are as follows:

Problem: One of the monuments (The Lincoln Memorial and the Washington Monument are referenced the most) in Washington D.C. is deteriorating.

Why #1: Why is the monument deteriorating?

Because harsh chemicals are frequently used to clean the monument.

Why #2: Why are harsh chemicals needed?

To clean off the large number of bird droppings on the monument.

Why #3: Why are there a large number of bird droppings on the monument?

Because the large population of spiders in and around the monument are a food source to the local birds.

Why #4: Why is there a large population of spiders in and around the monument?

Because vast swarms of insects, on which the spiders feed, are drawn to the monument at dusk.

Why #5: Why are swarms of insects drawn to the monument at dusk?

Because the lighting of the monument in the evening attracts the local insects.

Solution: Change how the monument is illuminated in the evening to prevent attraction of swarming insects.

7. The Servant

As I mentioned earlier, leadership is not complex. This does not mean that leading is easy, but it is not a complicated endeavor. For me, being a servant to my team is a critical trait and not a leadership style. Many would disagree with me on this as the servant style of leadership has become quite popular, but is not without its issues. The servant leader, as made popular by Robert K. Greenleaf, is the person who places the needs of his or her employees above the needs of the leader while solving any problems the employees may have. Remember the briefing on the airplane? Put your oxygen mask on first, before assisting others. I believe that being a servant is an ever-present quality consisting of six key words… what can I do for you? Practice it daily. How can I best enable you to do your job? Sometimes we should simply stay out of the way of our teammates and let them do what they know how to do. Other examples of serving those you lead include ensuring you have the right number of people on the team and everyone is properly trained to perform their primary task. It is also incumbent on the leader to ensure that everyone is properly equipped with any and all materials required to perform their primary role within the company. In the military we refer to this as: Title 10, US Code, Man, Train, and Equip. From an aircraft carrier, to a Naval Hospital, to an EOD Technician whose primary duties include diving, parachuting, and all things explosives, manning, training, and equipping is a primary function of any leader.

Serving those you lead does not mean that you are doing their job for them, it simply means that you are creating conditions for each teammate to thrive. In considering what conditions to create, you are leading at the strategic level. In serving those I lead, I often ask myself "what can I do to further enable others?" There are numerous books and podcasts on this simple subject. A simple search on Google will reveal volumes of discussion and a variety of definitions of servant leadership. As I mentioned earlier, leadership is a personal brand. As such, people define the varying aspects of leadership in different ways, which I think is great. Creativity in leading does not always mean uniformity. Serving others can take many forms.

8. Invest in Your Team

I have observed that far too many leaders do not budget time and funding for leadership development, especially among newer teammates and those in the lower ranks. Fast forward 10-20 years, and the organization has tenured people that are more problematic than productive as a great culture never really existed and resentment toward the organization and teammates developed. I have seen this in several companies with whom I have consulted.

Developing leaders at all levels is critical, as is developing leadership early in one's career. The two most obvious outcomes of investing in leadership development for new hires are that they will develop an empathy for what it is like to walk in their leaders' shoes, and they will think and feel that they are valued by the organization, which contributes greatly to the culture and values that we discussed in Chapter 1. Developing leaders at the lower levels within any organization will relieve mid and upper-level managers and leaders from the situations that can (and should) be handled at the lowest level possible, meaning you are increasing upper-level bandwidth. I have lived this method of leadership in the military and more notably in my private sector business. Developing leaders early in their careers enables effective delegation and empowers people to make decisions appropriate for their level.

Onboarding is an often-neglected process that if done properly, can empower a team-oriented mindset and plant the seeds of leadership within every new hire. My onboarding process requires that each new hire visit every office and every manager to learn about what that person does for the company. This is also where each manager mentions the three core values of the company, loyalty, integrity, and professionalism (hopefully you recall these core values from chapter one) and how our adherence to our core values continues to bring success while almost eliminating serious conflict. This also puts everyone on a first name basis which builds a bond between teammates. Our onboarding process is intentional, typically spanning 30 days or so to allow new hires to slowly take in all the information and new names while determining how to best serve the needs of the company and her crew.

Task-specific professional development is another area where forward thinking leaders spend time and money. Social media is the best example as of this writing. Although I hired people with social media expertise, major changes in social media platforms seem to occur daily. I often ask my Sales and Marketing team to find a course, school, or other venue that they can attend to advance their knowledge, skills, and abilities regarding all things relative to their areas of responsibility in the workplace. In a perfect world, everyone on the team, regardless of whether the team consists of two people or two thousand people, should have a professional development (PRODEV) pipeline. Once again, larger organizations have many PRODEV programs in place. They should make it a priority to "refresh" these programs from time to time.

One final aspect of investing in your team is to ensure that they have modern equipment and uniforms. Outdated equipment will slow the process, whatever the process is, and personal dress and grooming standards should be designed to reinforce personal and professional pride.

9. Challenge Assumptions

Challenging Assumptions is a sense-making technique designed to deconstruct a statement and discover where assumptions may be limiting your options. Far too often assumptions limit forward progress. This process is particularly useful when there is a "know it all" in the room. Challenging your own assumptions and those of others in the workplace is a critical thinking process that should lead to creativity, providing greater clarity regarding the issue. If your culture and values within your organization are high, and trust is established, people are comfortable both challenging other's assumptions, and having their own assumptions challenged. This leads to highly productive discussions that either validate the current assumption, advance the concept, or kill it. This is also a time when dynamic tension may occur. A mentor of mine described dynamic tension as intense disagreement without being disagreeable. This process works very well. At times, I will challenge assumptions to create dynamic tension. My team will challenge me from time to time and when they do, I love it. I have to prove my case, which sometimes reveals flaws. Challenging assumptions becomes easier and more productive the longer the team has been together. Referring to trust once again, we know we have each other's back. Or as my friend Dr. Gary McGrath calls it, I Got Your Back Leadership (IGYBL). If this high level of trust does not exist, challenging assumptions can be problematic.

10. Leading outside of work

Leading outside of work can be a most rewarding endeavor that pays big dividends at work and at home. Volunteering to coach youth sports, teach a skill such as music, or seek a leadership role in a 501-based foundation or association allows you to make a meaningful contribution to your community, positively impact the lives of others, and establish name and brand recognition. I recommend that you join your local Chamber of Commerce, which can lead to committee participation. While a Chamber of Commerce's mission is generally to advance the business environment, your time is donated. Seeking a leadership position within your local Chamber will increase your network while giving you and your business greater visibility. Leading a group of likeminded professionals will also increase your knowledge regarding all things business. We were fortunate enough to be selected as the Chamber of Commerce Small Business of the Year in 2018, and I was presented with the Chamber's Leadership Award in 2022.

Coaching youth sports has been a most rewarding process for me. If you have young children and you and your child share a love of a particular sport, coaching your child's team throughout their childhood years will be fun, rewarding, and will provide significant personal growth for you and your son or daughter. It is also quite rewarding to see all the other kids develop from 5 year old hockey players to young men and women excelling at the high school level and beyond. I have been coaching youth ice hockey for well over a decade. Coming up with my son through the age divisions in hockey, I am in my third year of coaching at the high school level. Thankfully, USA Hockey has strict coach training requirements as well as background checks for any adult participating in any aspect of facilitating youth hockey such as running the scoreboard and carpooling. Hockey coaches are required to complete extensive training, including age-specific modules based on the age of the team you are coaching. Each year I leave the coaching seminar feeling energized and ready for the upcoming season. These coaching seminars have also made me a better leader in my business, a better father, and a better husband. The interaction with the seminar facilitators leads to great book recommendations and other tools to further my ability to lead on and off of the ice.

11. Rehearse

Verb: practice (a play, piece of music, or other work) for later public performance.

Musicians rehearse, athletes train, scholars research, and developing your peak leadership skill is no different. In Navy EOD we would rehearse the mission. For a diving operation we would often "dirt dive" the plan, meaning that the EOD team would assemble on the pier or in an open area such as a field, and each member of the team would walk and talk through their role in the diving operation and how we will render safe the explosive device. The same holds true for military static line and freefall parachuting operations. We rehearse aircraft entry, procedures while in the aircraft, the aircraft exit, and emergency procedures (EPs) in the case of a parachute deployment malfunction. The more we practice, the more we rehearse, the more we refine our processes while developing muscle memory.

Rehearsal also can remove emotion and anxiety from the situation. The more times you are exposed to a certain situation, positive or negative, the less emotional you tend to be. I have over 1,000 parachute insertions (not a lot comparatively) and to this day each time I jump there is a tiny bit of anxiety. I speak publicly, and always rehearse my remarks prior to the event. My wife hears me talking to myself (rehearsing) in the shower, or while driving and she simply thinks that I am nuts. Rehearsal brings your executive functioning closer to its peak, and your ability to properly handle the situation is greatly enhanced. You may rehearse situations that are positive, negative, neutral, or something else. I rehearse engagements of all types to include, public speaking, upcoming business negotiations, one on one discussions with teammates, sales presentations, hockey practice plans, hockey game prebriefs, podcast and radio productions, and the list goes on.

We all think about upcoming engagements, but few of us stand in front of the mirror and rehearse. Video recording your rehearsal session is even better. A major production is not necessary for a rehearsal to provide great value. Hit record on your phone and stand in front of the mirror. Allow yourself several takes until you are happy with your presentation. Role playing is also quite productive. You can either be the role player helping a teammate or coworker prepare for an upcoming event, or you can ask someone to role play for your upcoming event. The feedback is almost instant meaning that significant improvement occurs quickly.

DRILL

1. Review the critical traits in this chapter and put a check by the ones that you are already doing. Circle the ones you would like to implement.

2. Think about experiences in your professional life that seem to occur repeatedly and develop your own critical traits to add to my list.

You may only have two or three to begin with...maybe only one. Add these traits to your Leadership Profile at the end of Chapter 3, and refine from time to time.

CHAPTER 5: READ AND REACT

BLUF: Find, fix, and finish these six daily leadership challenges

Read and react

On a night training jump mission in the Arizona dessert, I was the last of 22 military freefall parachutists to exit the Hercules C-130 aircraft from an altitude of 13,000 feet. I was one of the instructors for this training evolution, and in the blackness of the night sky I could see the relatively straight line of glow lights on the jumpers who exited via the tail ramp just seconds before I did. On a jump like this as we descend into the darkness, at a predetermined altitude the routine is to create vertical and horizontal separation by alternately changing our heading 90 degrees to the left, the next jumper 90 degrees to the right, and so on, until each EOD Technician deploys their parachute (canopy) at a predetermined altitude. Upon successful parachute deployment, each jumper activates a strobe light affixed to their helmet. On this night, I was the last jumper in the stick (group of jumpers, like a murder of crows), and could see the helmet strobe lights illuminating the canopies ahead of me, as they began to disappear in the distance.

Disappear? Wait. I am supposed to follow those strobe lights to the landing zone (LZ), but now I couldn't see a single one. Normally I would aim for a cluster of strobe lights as the rest of my team landed on the LZ. In this case, our "go" signal to exit the aircraft came seconds too late, and the jumpers ahead of me realized we had missed the LZ. They changed their heading to hastily establish alternate LZs. As they maneuvered to safely land off heading, it was clear to me that I better do the same. Not only that, but I was lost in the night sky. It was time to initiate emergency procedures by locating an alternate landing zone, and it would not be illuminated this time.

As I surveyed the rapidly approaching terrain beneath me, my training kicked into high gear. Our training directs that we avoid linear terrain features as this would most likely be power lines or roadways where the driver of a vehicle might hit you before they see you. Instead, we are trained to look at the terrain contrast and steer towards the lighter shade of black or gray in the hopes that it is *terra firma* and not a building, lake, pond, canal, or other body of water. These steps are the find and fix from our **BLUF**. As my altimeter indicated that I had about 100 feet of altitude remaining, I pulled on my brake lines and held them steady at 50% while bringing my legs together in preparation for what the military calls a parachute landing fall (PLF). This is the finish from our **BLUF**.

A PLF is a procedure where the jumper contacts the earth first with his or her feet, then rotates slightly to one side or the other allowing the calf to make contact next, followed by the side of the thigh, then the hip, ending by rolling through the lats (*latissimus dorsi*) just under the shoulder. At the same time, I closed my arms in front of my chest and head to help avoid injury. As this event unfolded, I was able to process the emergency procedures in my mind, leading to action, resulting in a successful landing in a horse pasture, narrowly missing a horse that I could not see in the darkness. This slow-motion process could have been terrifying, but I stayed calm and relied on my training, creating time to think, and time to apply the emergency procedure that was predetermined for this very situation.

Sometimes leadership can resemble being lost in the night sky. A leader needs to **read** the situation and **react** appropriately. This chapter gives you the tools to read and react accurately, and eventually more quickly.

Find, Fix, Finish

In military-speak, the F3EAD cycle (Find, Fix, Finish, Exploit, Analyze and Disseminate) is an intelligence cycle used in lethal special forces operations. We used F3EAD to locate and identify improvised explosive device (IED) makers, their factories, and supply routes. After a takedown of the facility and the terrorists, we would gather all information relative to what type of explosives and fusing materials they were using and when and where the next attack might occur. This information would be quickly shared.

During my 11 years in the private sector, and upon reflecting on my military career, I have curated the following six frameworks which help me to quickly read and react to daily leadership challenges. These issues seem to be ever present in the workplace. The first task is to *find* which of the following six challenges you are dealing with, the second step is to *fix* your aim—which direction am I going—then *finish* resolving the issue *vis a vis* recurring situations that lead to frequent discussions and actions across all five of Collins' leadership levels (Chapter 1).

If you lead an organization of any size, you will meet at least one of these six issues daily:

1. Performance vs. Behavior
2. Voice vs. Vote
3. Leadership vs. Management
4. Think vs. Feel
5. Step Up vs. Step Back
6. Culture vs. Climate

Before we break these down, let me explain why I chose to use "versus" in setting up this discussion. *Versus* reflects the inherent contrasts in each situation. As a leader, I need to first *find* which contrast applies to the situation, *fix* my aim within the contrast, and *finish* applying the appropriate solution. Similar to our discussion regarding my eleven critical traits, the six situations listed above could easily be expanded, but one or more of these six seem to present themselves daily.

Performance vs Behavior

Why are some people forgiven while others are fired for issues at work? Although we addressed this in Chapter 2, I will further address this question here. Our first situation, Performance vs. Behavior, answers the question with great clarity. I have found this to be one of the most valuable tools at a leader's disposal in making decisions regarding retaining, reassigning, retraining, or letting someone go.

As you know by now, I like to begin these discussions with definitions. Performance is defined as the execution of an action. For me, performance is measured by quality and/or quantity of work produced by the individual or the team. High performance should result in a high ROI. Behavior, on the other hand is simply one's moral and ethical character. It is a willingness to show up on time every day with a great attitude and give your employer and your coworkers your best. This great work ethic demonstrates <u>commitment</u> to the team and not just <u>compliance</u> (another contrast). In my experience, behavioral traits are developed throughout childhood and perhaps very early in one's professional life, meaning people either show up with a great work ethic, or they don't. The following visual representation makes the process more clear.

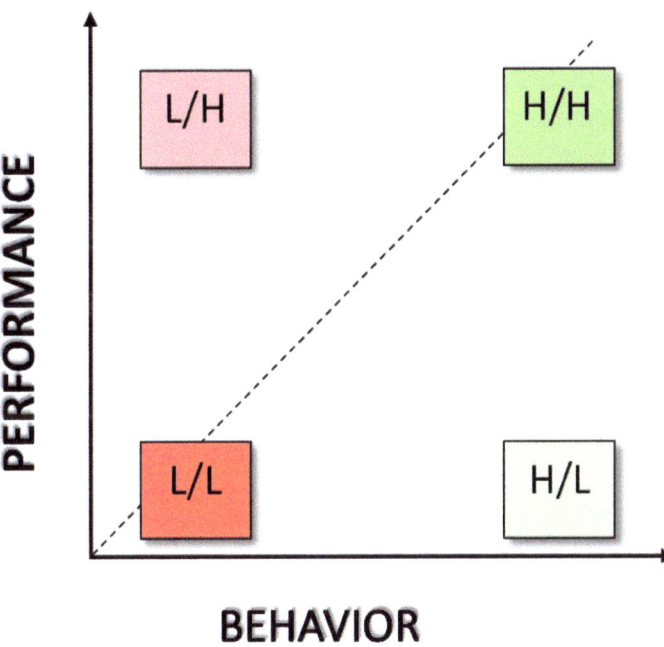

Let's begin with the easy approach to performance vs behavior. High-performance, high-character individuals are who businesses seek out. This should be the main purpose of an interview. I am less concerned about the four corners of a resume and more concerned about a potential employee's moral and ethical character. When you discover that you have a high-performing, high-behaving person on the team, reward the employee. Keep them on task and make sure their plate is full without overloading them. This is what high-performing, high-behaving individuals seek. They take pride in their work and feel satisfaction by making significant contributions to the mission of the organization and to their teammates. It is fun and rewarding to watch these people do what they do. They own it, all of it, and in doing so will likely make great contributions to the culture of the organization.

Ideally, all members of your team are high performing and high behaving individuals, but this is not always the case. Let's look at low performance and low behavior. This is also easy, they have to go. How did a low performing, low behaving individual get hired to begin with? If your HR or other hiring process hired this type of person, perhaps a review of the hiring process is in order. A low performance, low behavior person is a drag on the rest of the team, and often becomes toxic to the team. They will deliberately attempt to contaminate other teammates. They will blame others for their shortcomings and rarely accept responsibility. Once you have identified low performance and low behavior in someone, act quickly to terminate their employment. Perhaps you have heard the saying "hire slow, fire fast." My experience has taught me that this is good advice. In my consulting work, I am often surprised at how tolerant leaders are of low performing, low behaving individuals. It is usually better to leave a position unfilled than to tolerate someone who is not committed to the good of the organization and their teammates. Legacy Human Resources teaches that leaders should use progressive discipline. Experiences teaches that you should quickly terminate problematic people.

Now let's look at the two more difficult scenarios, a high performing, low behaving person, and a low performing, high behaving individual.

As leaders, high performance is what we notice more than anything else. High performance is great for ROI which is the mission of most commercial enterprises. However, high performance can often mask low behavior. Low behavior is poison, it is a toxin that will spread throughout the organization, ultimately undermining the efforts of leaders and business initiatives. Low behavior takes many forms and you will know it when you encounter it, and you must address it immediately. I was blinded by a high performing, low behaving person early in my private enterprise experience. When I finally let this person go, several others expressed support for this decision. I was also informed that others recognized the low behavior but thought I was giving this person a pass for other reasons. Several other smaller issues disappeared along with the person I fired. Eventually, a few other people, loyal to the terminated employee left as well. This was a pivotal experience that significantly improved workplace conditions for everyone else on the team. Our culture was reestablished, or redefined in a positive manner. Low behavior consumes precious time that is already in limited supply for leaders, as they address the individual's shortcomings. So, it is my experience that under any circumstance, a low behaving person has to go.

What about the low performance, high behavior teammate? This is the most challenging of the four scenarios. As I mentioned earlier, a high behaving person is what employers should be looking for. *Hire for behavior and train for performance.* When it is apparent that one of your teammates is under-performing, it is the leader's job to figure out why. We all have lives outside of work and sometimes one's personal life can interfere with job performance. I recommend a candid discussion with the under-performer to get to the root cause…the 5 Whys perhaps. For example, I had a US Navy Chief Petty Officer who worked for me begin to underperform. Upon questioning, we discovered that he had become very tired at work as of late, and he did not know why. He would doze off at a red light on his way to work in the morning. Upon discovery of a sleep disturbance, I referred him to the appropriate medical professionals who discovered that he had sleep apnea. After the underlying issue was identified and addressed, his high performance returned, and possibly his life was saved. In another scenario, I had an employee (we will call him Bill) who was a very good teammate to everyone and was very good at his craft. Then, Bill's lead instructor noticed that he had become somewhat complacent regarding safety and lacked adherence to the governing directives and manuals. His risky actions put the welfare of his coworkers and the company at risk, and everyone saw it. Why was this otherwise highly skilled team player performing recklessly?

When his team leader called him in for a discussion, Bill admitted that he had become reckless. He also admitted that he enjoyed the risks he was taking while at the same time he knew that he was letting his teammates and company down, and he felt the guilt of his actions. He thought that he was improving the experience of our paying customers, when in reality, they could not know any difference in the delivery of the product. In this situation, an otherwise high behaving teammate, his leader sent him home for 7 days to think hard about what the job meant to him and whether or not he wanted to continue employment with us. Bill's future was up to Bill. After the 7th day, Bill reported for work and indicated that he needed the time to work on himself and felt that he was ready to tighten things up. Bill took ownership of his recklessness, and genuinely wanted to correct the situation. Using this method of asking the employ to take time off (paid or unpaid, but usually paid) to solve their own problem has a good chance of success as long as they own the problem, which Bill did. Using this method on low behavior teammates will often result in them not returning at all, or calling/emailing to give notice that they will not be returning.

Sometimes, a high behaving individual has performance issues because the tasks they were hired to perform are simply beyond their capability. This is also a very difficult situation as high behavior is the gold standard for me. Almost anyone with great moral and ethical character has something to contribute to the team. When you have high behaving teammates who fall short on performance, you have three options. Train to the expected level of performance, reassign them to tasks where the level of performance is less stringent, or terminate. As the Officer In Charge of a Counter-Terrorist response team, I had to remove one of my men from an upcoming deployment due to lack of technical skill. This was tough to do as he was a great teammate, liked by everyone, very good at most of our skill sets, but when the stakes were high, he was unable to deliver at the level required to quickly and decisively identify and disable terrorist explosive devices, aka IEDs.

On another occasion more recently, I had to let a manager go. This manager was of the highest moral and ethical character but simply could not perform consistently at the leadership level required of the position. In both cases each person accepted the disqualification and owned their shortcomings which is perhaps the hallmark of high moral and ethical character. In my experience this is the most difficult scenario.

In situations where you must terminate a high behaving person, using this matrix and even sharing the process with others will make the termination more acceptable to everyone, particularly the person being terminated.

Voice vs. Vote

This contrast is quite simple to understand but can often get away from leaders. In my organization, all voices will be heard. If you have something to say and can present it in a manner that does not attack your teammates, I am all ears. If you think it is necessary to attack your teammates, experience tells me that you are probably wrong, but I will still listen. I want to hear from everyone, from the newest member of the team to the most seasoned. It has been my experience that the best ideas for product or service improvement come from the customer-facing folks, the front line, tactical level people who deliver the product or service. In the military, enlisted Soldiers, Sailors, Airmen, and Marines are the workforce and their voice is critical. Therefore, I what to hear from them often. We have all heard of the Good Idea Fairy. Not every idea is good or even executable, so I ask three questions when presented with ideas for change.

1. Will it enhance the employee experience?

2. Will it enhance the customer experience?

3. Will it enhance the bottom line?

If the answer is yes to all three questions, we are most likely going to do it. If the answer is yes to one of the three questions, we will look more closely at the situation to see if the concept can be further developed.

It is any leader's responsibility to hear from everyone under their charge. It is also the leader's responsibility to make decisions that are in the best interest of the organization first and foremost, and this does not include putting major decisions to a vote. Hiring, firing, allocation of dollars to budgets such as investment in professional development, marketing initiatives, facility improvements and renovation, travel, employ retention incentives, healthcare and retirement benefits...the list goes on. Accountability for decision making rests with the leader. You, as the leader of your organization, are expected to make decisions that are in the best interest of the organization. After receiving input from subject matter experts and others who may be impacted by the decision, you will make the best decision possible. Rarely do we have one hundred percent of the information we need to make a decision, but every situation reaches a point where it is decision time. Indecisive leaders hold up the rest of the team.

Is there a situation where a vote is in order? Sure. Items that make the workplace more accommodating such as what type of coffee machine, where to have the Christmas and holiday party, and other items that do not directly impact cardinal direction or profitability may benefit from a democratic process.

Finally, valuing all voices promotes an inclusive environment and is good for business. You will derive a more diverse demographic, be more innovative, responsive, and resilient to changing conditions.

Leadership vs. Management

This age-old discussion will never go away, nor should it. It is of critical importance for leaders to know the difference between leadership and management and when to apply each. While management is necessary in all work settings, it is distinctly different than leading. My friend Marty Strong (US Navy SEAL retired, CEO and author) in his book titled *Be Nimble*, and in our conversation on my podcast, describes leadership with a lower-case *l* in contrast to leadership with a capital *L*. The small *l*, or management, is monitoring preset conditions and parameters and implementing preapproved corrective actions to fix the problem, returning to within-parameter conditions. Managers have great technical competence. Leading people, on the other hand, requires a detailed understanding of the organizational goals and inspiring everyone on the team to pursue those goals with vigor. People want to be led, but not managed, and certainly not micromanaged.

As entrepreneurs, we start out as the subject matter expert delivering the product or service while developing and refining the business plan as the company's executive. Over time we have to evolve our leadership by not delivering the product or service directly, rather we should enable others to directly interface with customers while we create the conditions for our teammates to be successful. And finally, you have probably heard someone push back against high expectations with something like: "hey, I'm not a robot." It's true – your people are not machines.

It is critical that you lead, especially when a situation demands leadership. Those you lead have lives outside of the workplace. Many have partners, wives, husbands, children, house payments, unexpected visits to the emergency room, unanticipated expenses, illness, death of loved ones, and on and on. In some cases, such as the death of a family member, this will most likely be a life- changing event. In my experience, particularly in the military, your ability to lead the person and the organization through this life-changing event is one of the hallmarks of leadership.

The following is from a 2016 Forbes article:

Differences Between Being A Leader And A Manager (FORBES 2016)

Leaders create a vision, managers create goals.

Leaders are change agents, managers maintain the status quo.

Leaders take risks, managers control risk

Leaders are in it for the long haul, managers think short-term.

Leaders are unique, managers copy.

Leaders build relationships, managers build systems and processes.

Leaders coach, managers direct.

Leaders grow personally, managers rely on existing, proven skills.

Leaders create fans, managers have employees.

And on and on. A Google search on this contrast will reveal more information than you can consume. Referring back to Chapter 3, define leadership in your own terms and hold yourself to account. Those you lead will let you know if you are in the leadership zone, and if you are not. Seek their feedback when you think it would be helpful. This will also contribute to the high culture we discussed in chapter one.

Think vs. Feel

Like most of this book thus far, Think vs. Feel is as much about you understanding yourself as it is about you understanding others. In fact, the more and better you know yourself, the better you can lead and positively influence others.

Thinking, or thoughts, are linear and logical or illogical in my experience. Thoughts are of the mind or a function of the brain as the mind is not an organ and does not have a physical form. People will often state "I think we should…". The thought is a result of some type of observation or conclusion based on experiences that tend to be factual in nature. Or, someone on the team may say "I don't feel we should…"According to Joe Dispensa, in his book *Breaking The Habit Of Being Yourself*, feelings are the language of the body.. For example, "I think we should move ahead with the marketing campaign. A thought like this is likely based on the fact that the marketing campaign has been well developed, rehearsed, refined, and all makes good sense, creating great confidence in execution. Or, the statement could be "I don't think we are ready to move ahead with the marketing campaign." Again, this is likely based on observations and experiences that inform the person making the statement that all conditions have not been met. Often, the person making the recommendation may say "I don't feel we should move ahead with the marketing campaign." Or, "I feel we should execute the marketing campaign." Is this a thought, or a feeling, or both?

What's the difference? Do you, as the leader, care that much about a simple difference in someone's choice of words? Experience tells me that people will often express a thought as a feeling, and present a feeling as a thought. The value to you of knowing the difference is that when thought and feeling are in alignment, the chances of success are greatly increased. And, the opposite is also true. We have all felt, or sensed, that something was just not right, in various situations. This is where listening to your gut makes sense, and is worth a delay to review all relative information. Have you ever left your home, or work, or some other location and had the notion that "I feel like I am forgetting something?" then, long after you departed you remember the thing that you forgot that gave you that uneasy feeling. Remember, mono, stereo, surround sound…Now that you have addressed your thoughts vs. feelings, as you lead you will be better able to help people flush out their thoughts vs. their feelings. You will be more likely to accomplish your objectives faster and with greater accuracy. When the mind and body are in opposition consistency will not occur. When mind and body are in alignment confidence is heightened, decisions become clearer, any remaining fog may lift. Some may call this being "in the zone."

There is a lot of thought, feeling, and discussion about being an empathetic leader. Many would consider this to be a leadership style… not me. Being empathetic is a valuable trait of a leader but not a definitive leadership style. Why? Let's look at other emotions in this setting. Empathy, *em*, to be with or to be in with; *pathy*, to feel means *I feel with you…I'm in this with you.* In contrast, apathy is comprised of *a*, without and *pathy*, feeling…*I have no feeling for you* or *about* something. Finally, there is sympathy, *sym*, meaning "together." It is a regular occurrence in the workplace to send mixed messages by thinking one way and feeling another.

As you lead, know which *pathy* (em-, a-, or sym-) you should apply given the situation. It is generally very good to be empathetic. How to be empathetic…according to the Chriss Voss, in his book about the FBI hostage negotiating team (*Never Split the Difference*) is to listen…be a good listener. Listen intensely, demonstrating a desire to understand what the other side is experiencing. Use Tactical Empathy, active listening.

I like John Maxwell's three levels of listening.

- Level 1: Listening long enough for the other person to stop talking so you can say what you have to say.
- Level 2: Empathetic listening. I am here with you. I am in this with you.
- Level 3: Level 2 with the observation of body language. Do the words agree with the body movements?

You can significantly improve your ability to lead simply by listening in a very deliberate manner, not interrupting, asking questions, mirroring (using nonverbal cues to establish a rapport), and letting the other person speak until they feel that they have been heard.

Step Up vs. Step Back

This is not a complex discussion. Leadership is not rocket science and does not require complex mathematics. It does, however, require you to be present...to be in the moment. It requires you to consider all the angles and possibilities outside of the moment as well. Referring to our discussion about metacognition in Chapter 4, if you are using metacognitive processes, you will know when to step up and lead from the front, and when to step back and let others drive the effort or initiative. In fact, the more you can step back because you have developed trustworthy and competent subordinates, the better you are leading.

Once again, enabling others is a leader's primary role. My friend and retired US Navy EOD Master Chief, while attending *Elevate Your Leadership*, discussed how his father taught him that sometimes you lead from the front, sometimes you lead from the middle, and sometimes you lead from the rear. If the situation requires you to lead from the front and you are not there, woe unto you. If your team has things under control, yet you feel the need to assert yourself, woe unto you. When you have a high functioning team under you, try to position yourself in the middle, then move to the front or the rear as the situation dictates. Too much time in front will burn people out, including yourself. Too much time in the rear will create a loss of confidence with your team. Ultimately, your teammates will either fully support you, try to get you replaced, or resign. Let me say that again, your teammates will fully support you, try to get you replaced, or resign. Anything short of full support is unacceptable and must be addressed. I will add that when you find yourself leading from a less than optimal position, the sooner you acknowledge your error and adjust, the sooner your team will let you off the hook.

I have consulted with several companies whose leaders were not able to maneuver between the front, the middle, and the rear, and the issues they have are very similar from company to company. Those issues are likely to culminate in your subordinates attempting to have you replaced, or perhaps they will leave.

One final point of discussion here is when a business is family owned or family members have, or otherwise appear to have, privilege. There are two simple approaches here. First, treat all employees like family. Second, treat all family like employees. Good teammates will generally accept a degree of family privilege as long as they fully believe that you are focused on every teammate's wellbeing. On the other hand, irreparable resentment can develop quickly when an organization holds on to family members or other privileged classes who are not pulling their weight.

Culture vs. Climate

At various times throughout my military career, all crew assigned to a command were directed to complete a written survey, called a climate survey. This survey was intended to inform the higher level of leadership as to how a particular Commanding Officer was performing by measuring the morale of the troops, among other things. However, the climate survey did not take into account the culture of the unit/ command, which I contend is distinctly different than climate.

In every organization, culture is as present as climate, and has a much greater impact, in my experience. I am not downplaying the impact that climate can have as I know that the climate of any organization is of great importance.

To distinguish the two terms: climate is what you see while culture is the shared feelings and beliefs you perceive among employees. Climate is the neat and orderly appearance or the facility and the people manning the facility. Uniforms, personal grooming and hygiene, professionalism, and competence are all outward signs that create a mood we call climate. Climate is heavily influenced at the management level, but it is ultimately created and enabled by the highest levels of leadership.

Culture, on the other hand, refers to the feelings, beliefs and attitudes that employees share. Culture is deeper than climate. It includes the influence of the immediate environment on what people believe and value. Relationships within an organization have an immeasurable impact on culture. Culture is collaborative and defines acceptable and unacceptable behaviors within the organization.

Climate affects culture. Within my facility at iFLY Virginia Beach Indoor Skydiving, I am pleased to read comments on Trip Advisor and social media sites that mention how neat, clean, and well organized our facility is (climate). The comments usually go beyond and mention our great team and how well we all work together (culture). Most people, especially business owners and other leaders, can sense (think and feel) whether or not the climate and culture are thriving. Another example of climate would be "Dave and I work really well together." This professional working relationship fosters a great culture when the statement becomes "I love working here." Culture is an accumulation of positive experiences; the employee extrapolates from these discrete exchanges to an overall sense of satisfaction with the workplace.

From the beginning of this book I have emphasized the importance of defining key aspects of leadership in your own terms. Defining climate and culture gives you a clear goal to achieve, a goal that can also be realized by everyone in your organization. You can create the climatic conditions that will motivate your team to develop and maintain a thriving culture. To quote my friend and coach Bob Groves: **"culture is enabled from the top down and realized from the bottom up."** Everyone on the team owns the culture of an organization.

DRILL

1. Find a challenge that you face regularly and place it within one of the 6 contrasts (e.g., Performance vs. Behavior).
2. Fix your focus on understanding the problem through this framework.
3. Finish by addressing the issue head-on.

CHAPTER 6: DIVERSITY EQUITY AND INCLUSION

BLUF: . **The pathway to diversity is inclusion.**

In drafting this book, each chapter came with ease because my content and experiences are well developed and documented through my military experience, the Elevate Your Leadership program, professional articles, and the many podcasts I have been invited to as well as hosted. Although this chapter was not part of the original outline, the topic commanded national attention and was the first chapter to be fully addressed. In fact, it leapfrogged the other chapters. Why?

Over the past decade, and certainly catalyzed by the tragic death of George Floyd in 2020, the initiative of diversity, equity, and inclusion (DE&I) has gained renewed focus. Working toward improved DE&I is an inherent element of being a good leader—it simply makes sense. If you think you are already being inclusive, chances are you have good foundational principles in place. If you are feeling a bit ambivalent as we approach this discussion, rest assured you are not alone.

In addition to the timeliness of the topic for our nation, it has been a significant evolution for me as a leader to integrate my prior military experiences and expectations related to DE&I within the private sector. As an enlisted servicemember for 16 years, then as a commissioned officer for 10 years, my perspective on building and leading teams evolved. We made sure we paid attention to each other as teammates first. We never considered the color of skin as we executed missions—

it just wasn't a factor. The Navy core values of honor, courage and commitment apply to the ship, shipmates, and self in that order, and we swear an oath to uphold these values. Although these are not referred to as elements of DE&I, upon reflection, I realized our core values *are* DE&I—in action. While the military is not perfect, it is an excellent model and the most diverse and inclusive environment that I have ever been exposed to. How can you shape your business to infuse these values to advance DE&I? How can you make it your organization's standard practice, informing everyday work?

In my current role within the business community, and as a community leader and public figure, I witness DE&I initiatives gaining traction daily as companies, communities, and government agencies develop and implement DE&I programming. As I write this, I serve on the Hampton Roads Chamber of Commerce DE&I Committee, with the goal of developing DE&I initiatives that will further enable conditions for businesses to not only succeed, but to thrive. Certainly, DE&I can be difficult to get right, and I will admit that I am ambivalent regarding certain assumptions and beliefs coming from those who have been appointed as subject matter experts, but who may lack some critical boots-on-the-ground experiences in functional diversity and inclusion, as well as the business owner's perspective. This chapter has been developed concurrent with the DE&I Committee efforts. One of the tasks within the committee was to develop our own working definitions of each of the three words that encompass DE&I. We reduced each of the definitions to one sentence, making them easier to understand and execute.

Diversity: The characteristics that make individuals unique.

Equity: The process of allocating resources, programs, and opportunities to employees, customers, and residents.

Inclusion: The process of ensuring that every voice is heard, and all have a sense of belonging and are respected in the workplace, irrespective of their backgrounds.

DE&I in the military

I am dedicated to a diverse and inclusive work environment built on a foundation of 26 years serving the world's greatest Navy. My experience, especially within Special Operations, was one of diversity and inclusion. The sailor or soldier next to me was my teammate... literally a brother or a sister. We would die for each other if we had to. The memory of the young and brave people who I served with in Iraq will be with me forever. These young warriors were there to fight alongside me if need be, no matter what their heritage or skin color was, or job in the military. They knew it and so did I. For example, the admin clerk had a loaded weapon at her side while doing paperwork. She was trained and ready to use that weapon if necessary. Even before and after my time in the war zone, my experience with DE&I within the military was based on the core values of the services. The Navy and Marine Corps, for example, hold fast to the core values of honor, courage, and commitment. The Army's core values are loyalty, duty, respect, selfless service, honor, integrity, and personal courage. The Air Force's core values are Integrity First, Service Before Self, and Excellence In All We Do. General Ryan, USAF Ret., elaborates on these core values as follows:

> *Core Values help those who join us to understand right from the outset what's expected of them. Equally important, they provide all of us, from [the rank of] Airman to four-star general, with a touchstone—a guide in our own conscience—to remind us of what we expect from ourselves. We have wonderful people in the Air Force. But we aren't perfect. Frequent reflection on the core values helps each of us refocus on the person we want to be and the example we want to set.*
> *—General Michael E. Ryan, Chief of Staff, United States Air Force (CSAF), 1997-2001*

The US military has codified a set of core values that are constantly reinforced, and reinforce the standards for interpersonal actions.

Through this experience, DE&I has become part of my DNA. Is this adherence to common core values possible in society, writ large? To varying degrees, yes and no, but the outcome is somewhat dependent on early childhood experiences. We know that things like education and life experience add up to disparate lifelong trajectories. As I adhered to these values in establishing my business, I looked for ways that I could alter those trajectories for the better in my community. For example, my management team developed programming within our community to work directly with disadvantaged school children. In a very deliberate way, my team is going above and beyond to open doors and inspire students, developing pride and confidence in the next generation.

Enough said? Nope.

DE&I in the workplace

As positive as my experience has been with DE&I throughout my military life, there have been times when the outcome was less than ideal in the private sector workplace. I once had a female employee who was very interested in improving diversity and inclusion within our organization and was a very frustrated social justice warrior. She approached me with these frustrations, and I asked her to research and identify potential areas where we could improve. She spent five solid days on the task and returned without additional recommendations. I thought, *what a relief*, we had found our way forward together and could proceed with clear skies. This was not to be the case.

Months later, she continued to be frustrated, and began speaking out against the leadership team. We noticed rumors beginning to emerge on social media and were forced to consider the possibility that our public relations were being sabotaged from within. We talk about the importance of boundaries later in this chapter, but this experience highlighted the fact that not all DE&I advocacy experiences are successful. She was a warrior in search of an enemy, and she created a target within. At least that was my perception.

Instead of resenting her, as I perceived she resented me, I realized that her sense of mission was driving her to behave in these counterproductive ways, undermining her own credibility and ultimately jeopardizing her employment. My first instinct was, *she has to go*. I cannot employ a saboteur in good faith alongside other employees who depend on me and their teammates for their livelihoods.

On the other hand, what would terminating her do? Vindicate her resolve? Add fuel to her fire? Impress upon her that white males cannot be trusted, just as she had come to believe? Sanctify the overwhelming rhetoric filling the DE&I space? It was a no-win situation.

Or so I thought.

She did not have the benefit of experience in the workplace, as I had gained in the military and private sector, to appreciate the many layers that make individuals who they are. Perhaps this could be her defining moment, to be held accountable for corporate sabotage while being offered a path forward? What would you do?

It has taken me a while to come to terms with this situation. I deal with people in good faith. When this is not returned in kind, it is unfortunately no longer as surprising as it used to be. To resolve this unfortunate situation, I reflected on the core values of my organization. Loyalty. Integrity. Professionalism. Did I act in accordance with each at every step? Ship. Shipmate. Self. Yes, at every step of this difficult interaction, the leadership team adhered to these values. Unfortunately, the teammate in question did not want to reciprocate. There are times when actions demand consequences. However, if—in the service of advancing DE&I—you shrink from acting when the situation warrants, you lose credibility with your team and this affects your ability to carry out DE&I with fidelity.

While I disagree with the assertion of white privilege, I agree that it is more difficult for certain people to accomplish their objectives. As a business owner, my first priority in hiring is moral and ethical character because with these traits, competency can be developed. An employee's moral and ethical character, and competency, is not qualified by race, ethnicity, sexual orientation, and the many other diversity descriptors. At least it should not be, but the reality is hiring practices can allow demographics to creep into the decision matrix, introducing unconscious bias. For example, to consistently improve upon our DE&I initiatives, we are taking a close look at our hiring practices, including the basics of completing an application and interview practices. This tactical-level application of DE&I during the hiring process identified barriers to an invitation for interview. We are working on retooling our hiring process to meet individuals where they are, regardless of how their application was completed, to provide a more holistic review. I realize that my business is a laboratory within which we can work to improve DE&I and evaluate our progress in real time.

Inclusivity leads to diversity

As an employer of 40 people who depend on me for their livelihoods, I must make decisions that are in every teammate's best interest. In other words, I see my business as an organism needing certain elements to thrive, and I suggest that DE&I demands one thing of leaders: that we ensure all teammates have sufficient sunshine, water, and oxygen to flourish. If leaders can integrate DE&I fully in the workplace, the outcomes are fundamentally good for business.

However, I have also seen the topic of DE&I become mired in resistance because of how it is positioned in forums mainly because there is not widespread agreement on the definition and execution of DE&I. Universities have differing definitions as do federal, state, and municipal governments. Certainly, the DE&I initiative is born of the plight of racially, economically and socially oppressed groups, but as a leader who put DE&I to practical use while in uniform, I can attest first-hand that the true value to be realized from DE&I goes well beyond skin color. You may be asking, how is this accomplished?

I propose that you **focus on inclusivity first, before diversity**. This approach upends conventional thinking—that if you simply hire more women or more minorities you "fix" the problem—but I believe the inclusivity first model unlocks true and sustainable diversity and equity.

Refer to the last chapter on voice vs. vote. Put methods in place to ensure everyone's voice can be heard, especially by the leaders within the organization. It has been my experience that the best ideas come from the front lines, your customer-facing teammates. Not every idea is good, but the good ones often come from engaged teammates who want to help the organization succeed. Ideally, this includes every single person, regardless of skin color, background or experience, ability, education, or training. Rely on your employees' instincts and learn to be an empathetic *listener*.

A more inclusive organization has more room to maneuver. It is more innovative. It responds and adapts more quickly to changing demands, such as the COVID-19 pandemic we are emerging from. It is more responsive to all the voices around your table. By truly seeing and hearing everyone, your organization becomes *resistant* to the structural barriers that prevent promotion of the best ideas and people.

During an all-hands last week, I discussed how DE&I is owned by everyone in the organization. I opened with: "As a point of entry for our continued conversation on DE&I, I want you to know two things: 1) you have a voice, and we want to hear what you have to say, and 2) we are who we are because of you, and for us to diversify as we grow, we need you to bring more people to the table." Although it is incumbent on the leader to promote DE&I in the workplace, it is imperative that every team member act with inclusivity in mind as well.

Helping others fly.

I am committed to a diverse and inclusive workforce, and I come at it from a place of sustainable self-interest: if we make the best decisions possible for our businesses, we can do more for our employees and our communities which, in turn, creates a path to a more diverse workforce. Running a business requires us to make the absolute best decisions we can every day to secure the livelihood and well-being of every team member.

For example, Isaac is a young man who participated in our Seatack Soars program. Seatack Elementary is a school in a socioeconomically challenged area of Virginia Beach, VA. Each year for the 13 weeks before Christmas and the 13 weeks after Christmas, we host 12 fifth-grade students as an after-school program. Each Thursday the school bus brings us the 12 children at 3:30 pm. We feed and fly the kids at iFLY Virginia Beach, and we have a guest speaker discuss the many things in life there are to discuss. Over the 13 weeks I have the kids 2-3 times, and I teach them all about ice hockey as well. The program is designed specifically to develop great pride and confidence within each child. They see the instructors, they elevate their image of themselves, and they get out of their comfort zones a bit.

One day, their teacher asked the students to write about their career plans. I got an email that I will never forget. Isaac's teacher told me that he had written about wanting to become an iFLY instructor. Would Isaac have ever imagined skydiving instruction to be a possibility without our program? Probably not. My philosophy is that reaching out to the schools and neighborhoods of disadvantaged youths is a necessary and important aspect of DE&I, ultimately building an inclusive workforce. Not only will we develop capacity among young people to envision a different future, but we also set the example. My employees see that I place a high value on all people regardless of life experience or training. They see that I value individuals not only for who they are today, but who they have the capacity to become. Seatack Soars brings great pride and confidence not only to the fifth graders and their parents, but also to my team. We know we are positively impacting the lives of our neighbors, and our own kids. We love these kids and cannot wait to be there when they graduate high school.

Given the discussion thus far, I believe that employers are responsible to their organizations to hire competent people of high moral and ethical character. Skill sets can be trained, but moral and ethical character is developed throughout life. We can build workforce capacity through programs like this. The reality is, we all have challenges in our lives. "Something about school or life didn't work for me" is a challenge each of us must overcome. To be clear, some of us have had many more of these hurdles to overcome than others. The self-aware leader will look hard at what got in the way in his or her own life and seek to create opportunities for others. This is what we will turn to next—how to become more self-aware, and how to help your employees do the same.

Metacognition put into practice

In chapter 4 we introduced metacognition, the ability to observe oneself objectively. In this section we put it to practical use. Everyone in the company should take responsibility for personal limitations and cognitive biases.

In the ground rules of this book, the importance of leaving ego at the door was discussed. Through this discussion of metacognition in real life, we discuss strategies to ensure your team is fully engaged, running on all cylinders. While the importance of ensuring diversity in employment is widely accepted, progress has been throttled by a hyper-focus on hitting demographic targets while missing the power of a truly inclusive workplace. I will freely admit that I was not running on all cylinders in this respect when I launched my business, but I became more intentional as my vision broadened and I continue to evolve. The exercise of writing this book has contributed greatly to that broadening.

Upon establishing my business, the first few years were very focused on staying alive, making payroll, and solidifying a multi-year business plan. As we gained strength, my perspective broadened. I was aware of diversity and inclusion and already had a diverse workforce, but I wanted to learn more about how to measure and promote these values. I wanted our company culture to be inclusive because this had been my experience in the military. As mentioned previously, this approach was very much ingrained in my perspective: we did not spend a lot of time looking at the color of skin, hometown, accent, or gender. What mattered was keeping the team safe and completing the mission. The pressures of the battlefield can help forge this sense of cohesive teamwork.

In a business, however, it may take more intentional leadership to create the right environment for engaging all team members. I consulted with Helen Turnbull, PhD, author of *The Illusion of Inclusion: Global Inclusion, Unconscious Bias, and the Bottom Line* to gather more perspective on diversity and inclusion. Her insights were invaluable. When Dr. Turnbull describes the "illusion of inclusion" she references the pattern many companies experience: hire a diverse workforce with respect to age, gender, and race, but fail to achieve an inclusive environment where all members feel valued and engaged. Sure, they are at the table—Dr. Turnbull points out—but are they able to express their viewpoints or are they subtly ignored? Many organizations <u>hire</u> for diversity but <u>manage</u> toward similarity as employees are encouraged to assimilate. This may give the appearance of a cohesive workforce, but it may not fully develop an inclusive environment. Let us delve into barriers to true inclusivity, because as I proposed earlier, it is the key that unlocks a diverse and equitable workforce, and growth potential.

In a recent conversation with Dr. Helen Turnbull (visit my podcast to listen), we discussed her experience guiding global clients through the process of creating a more inclusive workplace culture. Dr. Turnbull has been working on diversity and inclusion for many years, yet she feels "…it's unfortunate that diversity and inclusion get put in the same sentence constantly." When we speak of diversity, we are talking about demographics: What's the gender diversity? What about race or cultural diversity? Age diversity? You can think of diversity as a hierarchy of characteristics shaped by these demographics, but individual characteristics are also important, such as creative talents, athletic ability, intellectual talents, foreign language, and unique life experiences.

For instance, when I was an instructor at the Naval Diving and Salvage Training Center (NDSTC), I was tasked with renovating our gym. A component of the renovation included graphics displayed on the walls. As I looked to contract someone with the necessary artistic skills, I noticed that one of my Navy Diving students had considerable artistic talent. I asked if he was interested in the task. There would be no extra pay, and it would likely require extra hours to complete. This young man (who happened to be Asian) stepped up to the challenge and did a great job. He received recognition for his efforts, and when I visited

NDSTC some 20 years later, his artwork endured. Stories such as this one should not be overlooked. The DE&I value lies in inclusive activities, among other items.

Is this evidence of diversity? Yes. The military is a very diverse workforce. But this may be a better example of inclusion. It is my belief that focusing on inclusion, giving everyone a voice, making sure all employees are valued, and utilizing every talent and experience they bring to the table is inherently good for your company. Through a concerted effort to develop and value your employees, guess what else you serve? Your core values—these employees become more loyal to you. The feedback loop empowers everyone. Inclusivity is what all good leaders do naturally. Let us return to my conversation with Dr. Turnbull and see what she thinks about diversity as differentiated from inclusivity.

> "Yes," Dr. Turnbull continued, "it goes deeper than those demographic characteristics. Inclusion pertains to the kind of environment in the workplace—do people feel valued? Do they have a sense of belonging? Do they believe their voices are heard? Are they actively engaged in their work? Or do they just want the day to end? Are they anxious? Are they committed to their work, or are they just counting the days until they can move on?"

True inclusivity begins with self-awareness. Dr. Turnbull has devoted her career to helping organizations identify the unconscious biases which hinder the full development of human relationships. Are you scheduling meetings in your own time zone only, or do you consider the needs of team members in remote locations? When you begin the meeting at 10am EST at your headquarters in Washington, D.C., do you say, "good morning"? Or do you also offer a specific greeting to employees in Tokyo, such as: "Good evening, and thank you for being with us at midnight in Tokyo, we appreciate your dedication to this project." Do you tend to chat with several team members before the meeting starts, unconsciously excluding several others from the banter? Do you tend to let certain people dominate the conversation flow during a meeting, or do you have mechanisms which ensure all members have an opportunity to be heard? During an interview, do you tend to favor someone with whom you feel comfortable?

These are examples of *affinity bias*, the tendency to gravitate to those with whom we are most comfortable. Do you modify your own style to align with the dominant culture in the room so that those in power remain comfortable? This is an example of *collusion*, a subset of affinity bias. These are several simple examples of our tendency to allow unconscious biases to direct our behavior. This can be harmless if we are in a neutral space, such as in our neighborhood. However, in the workplace it is important that the executives remember they are never in a neutral space. The boss always carries an invisible shield of power, and everyone is always concerned about what the boss thinks. This is a kind of affinity bias where you, as the leader, are the victim. People may behave differently around you, or be reluctant to provide honest information, because they want you to like them. Neutral space in the workplace simply means that you are not overlooking the voices of those with whom you lack an affinity bias with. For example, I may personally enjoy spending time with the operations team, or having lunch with the management team, but a leader who is DE&I-conscious will spend time with all others in the organization is some professional manner.

Consultants advise corporations to build an inclusive culture, but the rhetoric around inclusion is vast: fairness, respect, access, opportunity, space, voice, trust. Strategies to promote inclusion generally build respect and trust. Employees must witness that all individuals are treated with respect, and they must be able to trust that policies are implemented without bias. Regardless of the rhetoric, what holds a leader accountable for creating a truly inclusive workplace, though, is integrity. At iFLY, for example, our corporate values are loyalty, integrity, and professionalism. The golden thread running through all that we do is integrity.

Integrity asks: Are you behaving according to your moral code? Are you treating yourself with honor? It is the guardrail that ensures respect in our interactions with each other and builds trust among our employees because we hold ourselves accountable every day. Requiring that everyone be treated with respect ensures that all individuals are guaranteed a voice, opinions are valued, and loyalty is built. But does inclusion stop there? I would argue that we can take the value of inclusion one step further—inclusivity leads to growth and resilience in tough times, and we certainly have seen that this past year.

Check out what happens when you type "inclusion leads to" in a Google search bar. The search algorithm returns the most popular pages.

- inclusion leads to
  - inclusion leads to **innovation**
  - inclusion leads to **diversity**
  - inclusion leads to
  - inclusion leads to **growth**

Focusing on creating an inclusive corporate culture will naturally produce a more diverse workforce. How does inclusivity inherently lead to a more diverse workforce? By identifying and systematically filtering out unconscious bias at every level of operations, from customer service to hiring practices.

Identifying unconscious biases

Unconscious biases are the stereotypes or mental models developed over time and—as the term implies—can exert an unconscious influence on your decision-making. We all have unconscious biases, and this is not always negative or harmful. Perhaps an example would be helpful. You're a woman, alone late at night after enjoying a cocktail with friends, and you're walking back to your car. You hear a car pull up behind you, then begin to move slowly, following you as you turn down a sidestreet. Your gut says, this is unusual and you hurry to your car. On the other hand, an example of less-than-helpful unconscious bias might be walking into an urgent care clinic—do you expect the nurse to be female? Or you are about to have a technician come to work on some equipment. Did you consider that the technician might be female? A corporate tech security manager is on the way, do you naturally assume it will be a man? When you board a plane, do you imagine the pilot to be a tall, silver-haired, white male?

These unconscious biases can influence hiring decisions if they are not managed carefully. One way to make a pragmatic change in hiring practices is to remove all opportunities for bias to influence the progression from resume submission to interview. For example, consider how your applicants are processed. Are you aware of their name and stated gender from the outset? If so, you have already introduced the opportunity for your brain to take shortcuts and inadvertently advance those you might feel most comfortable with to the next phase of the hiring decision while excluding others. These subtle biases may filter out highly qualified individuals based on the very characteristics which might help improve your organization's diversity.

Relationships are important in the workplace, but the effective leader must be aware of the role of unconscious bias and rely on integrity to serve as a constant guardrail. In practice, what does integrity do for you? It forces you to operate with metacognition, as discussed in Chapter 4. You might ask yourself—am I giving of my time and interest without bias? Is anything in my typical daily routine creating an unconscious bias toward certain relationships? For example, it might mean ensuring that when you do a walk-through at midday, ask yourself—do you tend to walk through the building with the same route every day, thus spending more time with people at the start of your route and cutting conversations short at the end because you are eager to get back to work? Could you vary your route so that the employees feel equally valued?

Again, unconscious biases are not all bad. Dr. Turnbull equates them to cognitive shortcuts that have served a useful purpose in keeping us safe. The amygdala, a small portion of the brain that regulates your fight-or-flight response may have kept you alive on many occasions. It might have been the urge which rushed you to your car when you sensed you were being followed, or prevented you from stepping out into the street in front of a car that just sped around a corner. Unconscious biases can become a problem when their reflexive nature causes us to make decisions that exclude people based on factors not directly related to job performance.

One way that happens is through affinity bias, as discussed previously. We tend to socialize with people at work with whom we have much in common, perhaps a shared love of football or cooking. This is ok in a neutral space, like your neighborhood, but in a workplace, there is no neutral space when you are the leader. Everyone is watching, all the time. In a meeting, it is up to you to frame the conversation to ensure that all voices are given a chance to be heard. It may be that your female executive is very loquacious. She dominates the meeting while your quieter male engineer struggles to articulate a product concern. In the tech industry, having a female C-Suite executive is an important marker for diversity, but if she is dominating the rhetoric, excluding the voice of your product engineer, is this good for business?

Boundaries can protect inclusivity

Boundaries and clear expectations still serve an important role in preserving equitable access, voice, and removing the perception of impropriety. In other words, you do not want people to think you are listening to them simply because they check a "diversity" box. In fact, equity is best served by sound business practices, and appropriate boundaries which protect your employees from the perception of impropriety or undue access.

For example, if someone needs a ride from the mechanic to work, do not hesitate to offer a ride. But refrain from offering a ride every morning or developing a relationship outside the workplace which will give the impression of undue influence in the board room. Maintain appropriate boundaries around access to information and decisions. For example, create a neutral space at work for people to present opinions, ideas, suggestions, and complaints. Although some companies rely on anonymous suggestion boxes for this kind of feedback, I believe it is important to cultivate an environment of trust, which makes it possible for all voices to be heard directly, and without fear of reprisal. That is true inclusivity.

Boundaries also promote inclusivity by ensuring all voices are heard. Some practical strategies to ensure an inclusive meeting structure are to identify a person responsible for moving the conversation around the table, specifically allocating time to each department, and soliciting feedback in writing prior to the meeting. When power and privilege are not actively managed, people can start to form impressions that associate demographics with disparities in treatment or attention in public venues, such as during meetings or even casual conversations. Being aware of and managing unconscious bias can prevent these fissures from developing in your organization.

Yes, people can form assumptions, including negative ones, that are not an accurate assessment of how you think and feel. An example may be illustrative here. I have a wonderful young man who works for me. We have three floors in my building. This young man works on the second floor. I was walking across the second floor one day, and something was on my mind. I did not even notice anybody. I was just going from point A to point B, thinking about a problem I needed to solve. Apparently, my intent gaze caught this young man's eyes. I was unaware that I had even looked at him, I was so caught up in my thoughts. I found out later that he assumed I was upset with him. He went to a supervisor, and he said, "Why is Bob mad at me?" The supervisor immediately came to me and asked me if I was upset with the young man. Honestly, I didn't even know this employee was working that day. I am glad he looked into it rather than let something fester. Dr. Turnbull helped me work through this situation in our conversation:

> "Bob, if you think about that young man, and what he projected onto you, rightly or wrongly, he's drawing on data. He's drawing on data from you being in a power position, you're the owner of the business, he knows it's important to his job, that you are okay with him. And so therefore, you walk around with an invisible shield of power and status that you don't always realize you're carrying. So, everyone else in the organization is adjusting to see am I okay with Bob today?"

That is a key point: people are always wondering what the boss thinks about them.

> "Right, when you add the layer of complexity around race, or gender or sexual orientation on top of these everyday interactions, then every time you grimace and it's in my direction, I've got all this data not just from you, Bob, but from life in general."

There is a level of consciousness that everybody must have. I need to be conscious of how other people might be perceiving my interactions with them, and others should have a similar consciousness as these biases regarding those in leadership positions are also problematic. By educating your team you will increase everyone's awareness and reduce the incidence of unconscious bias having a negative impact.

Blind spots

In summary, it is important to remember that we all have blind spots, the key is to recognize them and avoid being defensive when they are pointed out. Your car may have a blind spot warning on the side mirrors. This chapter reminds us to simply check our blind spots as we develop an inclusive work force. Blind spots do not mean we are bad people. Our brains are hardwired for self-interest and similarity. We are all wired for survival. But we must catch the blind spots. In fact, in my organization, we have a phrase I call "challenging assumptions." I *want* my team to challenge my assumptions, I *want* them to let me know when I might be getting ready to make a poor decision. To do this, I must be approachable, relationships must be built on mutual respect, and we must possess a very high degree of trust among all team members. Highly functional trust takes some time to build. When the team realizes that we are all here for each other as much as we are here for the organization, trust can be put to work.

Now, that is the ideal, but teams do not generally start out that way. People must learn to talk to each other. I have seen this come to fruition both on my team, and within the Chamber of Commerce Committee on DE&I. We have developed a sense of trust and shared mission. Initially I was slightly concerned about walking on eggshells within the committee, however, the committee put me at ease. Our discussions now are highly productive and we take full advantage of the opportunity to really hear each other. The conversations have evolved with time, and we can now discuss DE&I at the strategic, operational, and tactical levels.

Within my own organization, it is the responsibility of each team leader to develop trust. For example, our core values are loyalty, integrity, and professionalism. When a new employee onboards, I have a conversation about these core values. But I always close with integrity, because if the new employee forgets the other two, a focus on integrity will ensure that the rest comes through. If we act with integrity, we encourage the difficult conversations that promote inclusion, and we can avoid walking on eggshells. As teammates, we look for opportunities to help each other out, lift each other up, and call each other out when we think a teammate may be deviating from true North. With integrity as our guiding force, we do not have to be afraid of conversations about inclusivity, nor do we tend to become defensive or operate strictly from the perspective of a group identity. We stay the course by becoming allies and advocates for each other, regardless of our demographics. The pathway to true diversity is inclusion.

DRILL

1. Develop and deliver a DE&I survey. The more your team contributes to and owns DE&I initiatives, the greater your chances for growth.
2. Have DE&I discussions during your walk-arounds, and during your routine meetings.
3. Challenge DE&I assumptions that do not clearly serve the ship and her shipmates.

PART II: THE SCIENCE OF LEADERSHIP

BLUF: Improve Your Health - Improve Your Wealth

The General Leadership Law states that Rest, Hydration, Nutrition, Exercise, Brain and Heart Health, and Lifelong Learning are so interrelated that a change in one, positive or negative, will have a corresponding change in all of the others and will directly impact your ability to lead.

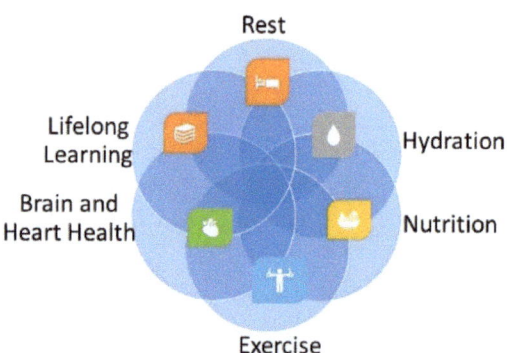

Now that we have completed our discussion regarding the art of leadership, we will move into what I believe is the most relevant aspect of leadership...Health and Wellness, which I equate to the science of leadership, hence, the General Leadership Law above, which I developed in 2019 after an epiphany. You should be energetic and clear minded throughout the entire day. In the following short chapters I will closely examine six aspects of science that greatly impact your ability to lead in the near, mid, and long terms. As is the case for the previous chapters, the following discussion is based on experimentation, events, and observations of my entire adult life and professional career in both elite Navy Special Operations and the private sector. Education, training, and experience all contributed to my ability to understand, harness, and present this critically important information to you. I also had the great privilege to attend a veteran's brain health program at The Marcus Institute for Brain Health in Aurora Colorado, a program designed for veterans with Traumatic Brain Injuries (TBI) and Post Traumatic Stress Disorder (PTSD). Although my diagnosis only found successive concussions (the mildest form of TBI) the treatment is designed to address mild cases such as mine as well as much more severe forms of TBI and PTSD. Several veterans in my cohort clearly had more severe signs and symptoms, and the incredible work of the Marcus team significantly improved everyone's quality of life, to say the least.

I have to take a moment here to state my deepest appreciation for The Boot Campaign, Virginia High Performance (VHP), and the incredible team of health care heroes at The Marcus Institute, which was established by a donation from Bernie Marcus, Home Depot co-founder. The three-week Intensive Outpatient Program (IOP) that I attended was life changing. Much of what I discuss in the chapters that follow is what I learned, relearned, validated, and awakened to during my visit. If you want to have high energy, mental clarity, and feel great about just about everything, read the following pages as if you are receiving the operating instructions for the rest of your life.

Let's define science right out of the dictionary.

Science: the intellectual and practical activity encompassing the systematic study of the structure and behavior of the physical and natural world through observation and experiment.

Let's simplify that a little bit. The study of the structure and behavior of the physical and natural world through observation and experiment. Folks, we are part of the physical and natural world. If you observe and experiment with your personal definition of leadership, your leadership style, and your power types, your ability to lead will become better and more effective and last for the long term. So, the science of leadership, as defined by me, has six major components. Those components are rest, hydration, nutrition, exercise, brain and heart health, and lifelong learning. There are four conditions under which we tend to make poor decisions. When we are hungry, angry, lonely, and tired (HALT), our executive function is reduced.

Executive function is a set of mental skills consisting of three main components. The first is your working memory which includes things like following the rules of a game, performing mental math, completing items on a checklist in order, and remembering details of a story. The second is practicing self-control which includes aspects such as patience and waiting, performing work without distraction, and sharing willingly. The third component is mental flexibility, represented by your ability to change modes from work to play, to mealtime. Mental flexibility also includes solving math problems, creative thinking and brainstorming, and adapting to change while accepting new experiences. I simplify executive function into three things: your ability to see, hear, and think.

By deliberately addressing rest, hydration, nutrition, exercise, brain and heart health, and lifelong learning on a daily basis, we can all but eliminate the conditions of HALT and maintain a higher level of executive function for longer durations.

On the page that follows, I created a very basic wellness worksheet. The intent is for you to personalize your approach to, and practice of, health and wellness as you read each chapter that follows.

WELLNESS WORKSHEET

Rest/Sleep

- Average daily hours of sleep last week: _____
- Average resting heart rate: _____
- Average sleep score: _____

Hydration:

- 16 ounces first thing in the morning
- Ounces of water daily: _____
- Number of ___ oz bottles of water daily: _____

Nutrition:

- Diet type
- Body type

Exercise:

- Maximum Heart Rate =

220 – (your current age: _____) = _____

- 60% of your maximum heart rate = _____
- 85% of your maximum heart rate = _____
- Minimum of 5, 30-minute, sessions per week
    - Run
    - Walk
    - Swim
    - Bike
    - Yoga
    - Weights
    - Other

CHAPTER 7: SLEEP

BLUF: Hi-performance leaders get enough sleep.

Did you know that sleep disturbances cause memory loss and irritability? Insufficient sleep and fatigue lead to poor judgment, lack of self-control, and impaired creativity.

If you are not well rested, you are not on your A game. When leaders lose sleep, their employees' experiences and output are also diminished.

HALT. Studies have found that when leaders show up for work unrested, they are more likely to lose patience with employees, act in abusive ways, and behave unethically.

How much sleep do you get every 24 hours? How much should you get? Do you wake up feeling well rested? Or do you wake up feeling sluggish? Why? Do you vary your sleep patterns on weekends?

Most literature regarding sleep is in agreement that preschool aged children (3-5 years old) require 10-13 hours of sleep per day, school aged children (6-12 years old) require 9-12 hours of sleep per day, teenagers (13-18 years old) need 8-10 hours of sleep per day, while adults need 7 or more hours of sleep per day.

The following is from my sleep app, CBT-1 Coach. Several research studies have shown that sleep is a process made up of two states: Rapid Eye Movement (REM sleep) and Non-Rapid Eye Movement (non REM) sleep. Non REM sleep is composed of several stages, and occupies about 75- 80% of the night's sleep of a "typical" young, healthy adult. The rest of the night's sleep is REM sleep.

Non-REM sleep consists of three sleep stages (N1, N2 and N3) that differ in their brain-wave activity patterns, perceived depth of sleep and in how much effort it takes to wake a person up.

N1: People experience stage N1 sleep as very light; when awakened, many individuals think they have not been asleep. Nonetheless, stage N1 seems to be an essential part of normal sleep. People with insomnia and older adults spend more of their night's sleep in stage N1 than those without insomnia.

N2: This stage occupies about 40-55% of the night's sleep in a young adult. It is harder to wake a person from this stage and most people know they have been asleep.

N3: Brain activity during N3 sleep is also called slow-wave sleep because it is characterized by slow, distinctive waves called Delta waves. N3 is perceived as the deepest sleep; it is hardest to wake people up from this stage. People tend to have more stage N3 sleep on nights following prolonged wakefulness. This is also the phase of sleep when growth hormone is secreted (this may be helpful if you're trying to convince your children to get to sleep!).

REM: REM sleep is when most dreaming occurs. During REM sleep, bursts of rapid eye movements can be observed and heart and breathing rates become less regular. There is increased blood flow to the brain. Interestingly, brain wave activities during REM sleep are a bit similar to those seen during wakefulness. However, during REM sleep the body's skeletal muscles are in a state of relative paralysis which prevents people from 'acting out' their dreams.

Through all of my *Elevate Your Leadership* courses, I've found that most people think they get somewhere between seven to nine hours of sleep every night, which is what most sleep researchers recommend for the average adult. However, your FitBit's sleep data may suggest otherwise. And there is always that one person who is proud that he or she can fully function on just 3 or 4 hours of sleep. I am not that person. Several studies have discovered a direct link between lack of sleep and the onset of dementia and Alzheimer's. Former US President Ronald Reagan, and former British Prime Minister Margaret Thatcher were both known to survive on little sleep. Reagan died of Alzheimer's-related pneumonia, and Thatcher suffered dementia after claiming that she got four hours of sleep per night while she was in office.

Even if you are getting enough sleep, research suggests that your team may not be. In fact, an international study conducted in 2017 by the Center for Creative Leadership found that 42% of executives got 6 hours of sleep or less each night. This chapter discusses the physiological benefits of good sleep, every night, but the effects of a well-rested management team extend beyond your own personal performance gains. Your energy and ability to connect and inspire, improves. You will also be more patient with your team and drive sustained engagement at work. All of these benefits are synergistic.

Your performance at work is a clear indicator of your sleep patterns. Picking up on patterns may help you anticipate your need for rest. For example, do you change your sleep cycle on the weekends and experience jet lag on Monday mornings? What days do you wake up and feel like you got a great night's sleep? Maybe you play a sport and are wound up when you get home, making the next day a bit tough. My high school hockey team practices at 9 pm during the week. After practice, it takes me a few hours to unwind which interrupts my normal sleep cycle.

Capturing the answers to the above questions will enable you to refine your daytime and evening habits, enabling a more restful and recharging sleep. Using a sleep app to record and review the various aspects of your sleep can be quite enlightening. Most sleep apps guide you through the process of learning about sleep, developing good sleep habits, and getting rid of behaviors that interfere with sleep. The sleep app I recommend is one that was provided to me by the great team at The Marcus Institute. It was developed by the Veteran's Administration for veterans and others who are participating in Cognitive Behavioral Therapy for insomnia and is free to download. It is called CBT-i Coach. It can augment treatment by a health care professional, or it can be used by you without the assistance of a health care provider. In roughly 20-30 minutes, this app will teach you more about sleep than you ever thought there was to know such as three conditions for great sleep: dark, cool, and quiet.

In addition to this and other apps, fitness watches and other health monitoring devices have become quite popular, and quite accurate. I use the Garmin Fenix Pro Solar. The following graphs reveal my sleep patterns and my corresponding resting heart rate.

As you take a look at the graphs, do some detective work based on the following information.

Alcohol can decrease time in REM sleep, reducing sleep quality. Travel to a different time zone or altitude can influence sleep quality and increase heart rate.

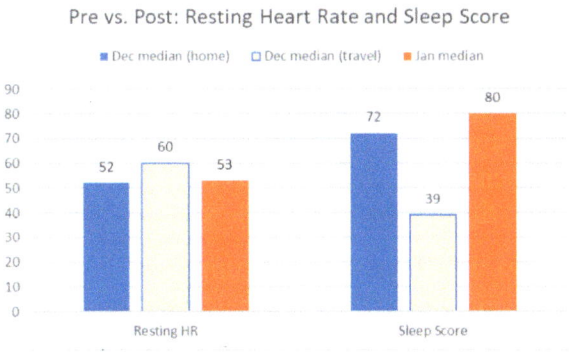

- When did I take a snowboarding trip to Utah?
- When did I do a dry month and avoid alcohol?

I traveled to Utah in December. Note that my resting heart rate is higher, and my sleep score is lower (light yellow). Studies have clearly demonstrated that we do not sleep as deep when we are traveling. In January my resting heart rate reduced to my usual 7 day average of 53 BPM, and my sleep score was eight points higher (80). I also refrained from alcohol in January, as I have for most of my adult life.

Even if you have developed great habits and routines to enable restful and recharging sleep, there are occasional nights where, for one reason or another, we do not get restful sleep and we know it when we are at work. We can feel it, and we can see it in the mirror. Eating and consuming alcohol or other non-alcoholic beverages within 2-4 hours of bedtime can interfere with restful sleep as your digestive system is working hard during your initial stages of sleep.

Applying the ground rule of mono, avoid making important decisions, and certainly avoid making urgent decisions where there is a lot on the line if you are not well rested. An unrested leader is not prepared for the challenges of the day. Perhaps you can take the day off, or delay decisions until you feel well rested and mentally energetic. You may be in a multi-day haze…it happens. I remember a marketing decision I made a few years ago that I later regretted. The pressure was on from the sales representative, I was tired and in a trough. The very next day I said to myself, "what was I thinking?"

Stereo…recognize when those under your charge are not well rested. While many leaders may think that an employee who did not sleep well or stayed out too late is not their problem, I assure you: it is the leader's problem. If you are the leader, it *is* your problem. Unrested teammates will be less productive and may not represent the company in an optimal manner when it really counts. Be prepared to address this with your teammates. If the problem is persistent as it was with the Navy Chief I discussed in Chapter 5, Performance vs Behavior, refer your employee to the appropriate healthcare professional.

Referring back to the General Leadership Law, in order to improve your quality and quantity of sleep, you must be well hydrated, eat properly, exercise regularly, monitor brain and heart health, and learn more about restful sleep as you are doing now.

I am certainly guilty of staying out too late and not being on my A game the next day. The military is famous (or infamous) for sleep deprivation. Basic training includes denial of sleep as a condition of the work environment. Military culture largely accepts sleep deprivation as a normal part of life on duty. Combat operations can create situations where inadequate sleep becomes the norm, but often military mishaps can be attributed to lack of sleep. While on deployment, military leaders should be conscious of the amount of sleep the troops are getting. In EOD and diving, especially while rendering safe (disarming) explosives, lack of sleep can have a catastrophic effect. I wish I would have learned this lesson earlier in my career as it takes great discipline to realize the value of the General Leadership Law, not to mention execution.

Brain chemistry

It is time to introduce the first two of four hormones that I will discuss in the remaining chapters. The brain releases these hormones throughout the day and night and they are critical to maintaining a high level of executive function. The remaining two hormones will be discussed in subsequent chapters.

- *Melatonin*

Melatonin is first up. Melatonin, often referred to as "the sleep hormone" is a hormone that your brain produces in response to darkness. It helps with the timing of your circadian rhythms (24-hour internal clock) and with sleep. Being exposed to light at night can block melatonin production. In order to enable plentiful and restful sleep, allow melatonin to do its job. There are many melatonin dietary supplements available, but it is best to enhance your natural production of melatonin through proper hydration, nutrition, exercise, brain and heart health, and lifelong learning. We want melatonin to help us fall asleep. One way to enhance this is not create conditions at bedtime that would counter the effects of melatonin, such as bright lights, caffeine, alcohol, or activity that elevates your heart rate.

- *Human Growth Hormone (HGH)*

The second hormone, human growth hormone (HGH) is secreted early in the sleep cycle, during slow wave sleep, usually before midnight. HGH heals your body and enhances physical growth. It plays a vital role in cell regeneration, growth, and maintaining healthy human tissue, including that of the brain and various vital organs. Deep and restful sleep produces the largest quantities of HGH.

Two final things on sleep and rest. First, inadequate sleep leads us to over-caffeinate, skip exercise, eat poorly, and underperform. If you are sleeping well, recharging, and have high energy and mental clarity most days, congratulations. As with most things, minor improvements in your sleep habits can have major effects.

Hi-performance leaders get enough sleep.

DRILL: Download a sleep app and use it diligently for 30 days. Make careful observations on day one such as how energetic and clear-minded you are throughout the day and make comparative observations every week for the full four weeks. Share your results with your teammates.

CHAPTER 8: HYDRATION

BLUF: Dehydration is an invisible enemy.

Factor number two in the science of leadership... hydration, or dehydration. Dehydration occurs when our bodies are not consuming enough water or fluids to account for the water lost. Dehydration, when combined with a lack of restful sleep, can have a cumulative effect which negatively impacts your executive function. Although our bodies process and lose water at a baseline rate that generally aligns with our metabolism, we can lose fluids at higher rates when we are sick, exercising, sweating heavily, or suffering from other conditions that result in the loss of excess amounts of water. Did you know that dehydration increases heart rate and reduces executive function? Dehydration causes strain on your heart. The amount of blood circulating through your body, or blood volume, decreases when you are dehydrated. To compensate, your heart beats faster, increasing your heart rate and causing you to feel palpitations. Also, your blood retains more sodium, making it tougher for it to circulate through your body. Dehydration can be especially dangerous for children and older adults. If you are feeling ill or have symptom of a cold or flu, extra hydration is required. The best way to avoid dehydration is to drink water before you get thirsty, and water has zero calories. If you're thirsty, you're already mildly dehydrated. Most of us awaken in the morning in a state of dehydration.

Losing as little as 1.5% of your body's water, can cause symptoms which, for adults, include extreme thirst, less frequent urination, dark-colored urine, fatigue, dizziness, and confusion. While in the Navy, we used the color of urine test almost daily.

Hydration is defined by the American Academy of Health Sciences as the consumption of any fluid that does not contain alcohol. Coffee, tea, soda (fortunately or unfortunately) all contribute to hydration. Once again, any non-alcoholic beverage is considered hydration. Going forward, I will limit my discussion of hydration to focus on water only, although some would consider Bud Light as a hydrating fluid.

Roughly 60% of the human adult body is water. Your heart is 73% water, blood 83%, brain 73%, lungs 83%, muscle tissue 79%, and your skin 84%.

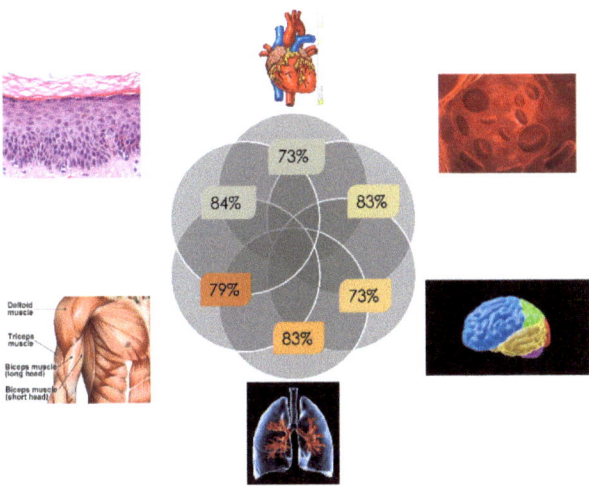

Proper hydration reduces muscle fatigue, improves lubrication, clears the skin, and boosts the brain resulting in greater productivity. So, how much water do you drink on a daily basis? How much water *should* you drink on a daily basis? Most people don't know the answer to either of these questions. Let's start out with the ideal scenario. Now, there's a bit of disagreement on this, but I have found the following formula to be the most credible. Divide your bodyweight, in pounds, by two, and that is how many ounces of water you should consume daily. For example, I weigh 180 pounds so I should drink, at a minimum, 90 ounces of nonalcoholic fluid on a daily basis. Do I drink that volume every day? No. That leads to question number two, how much water do you drink on a daily basis? Most people don't know the answer to this question because it requires you to meter your fluid consumption. The easiest way to meter your fluid intake is to consistently use a container that has a known quantity. For example, my Nalgene bottle is 32 ounces; I have to fill that water bottle three times a day to consume my daily recommended amount of fluid. If I exercise, which I do every day, I should consume more, and so should you. I have a 32-ounce Nalgene at home, and in my office. I also add a few rocks of Himalayan Pink Salt to my first 32 ounce bottle of the day to help maintain my electrolyte levels.

Not convinced that water is connected to cognition? A recent meta-analysis[1] found that approximately half of the studies were able to document rehydration linked to improvements in executive function. In another study[2], Ganio and colleagues did a treadmill dehydration test to estimate how much cognitive function is affected. They put a group of twenty-six, 20-year-old men on a 40-minute treadmill walk at 5% grade in an 80-degree room. The group was divided into three test conditions, treadmill plus: diuretic (to push fluids out), placebo, and rehydration. The mildly dehydrated men experienced degradations in vigilance, working memory, anxiety/tension and fatigue.

Most people are in a constant state of dehydration.

Dehydration, when combined with lack of sleep, has a cumulative effect which begins to impact your executive functioning. How does this apply to leadership? Quite simply, it is one of the six factors that contributes to poor decision-making and lack of situational awareness. Dehydration is the silent enemy that stalks you. Sometimes we eat when we are actually thirsty HALT. Rarely does an alarm go off and trigger a thirst reflex, like the feeling of coming off a long run on a humid day, drenched in sweat. Clearly: water needed. If it's mid-afternoon, you have eaten lunch, you're more likely to need water than food. Start with 8 ounces of water then see how you feel in 20 minutes. What is the benefit of assuming hydration is the issue instead of hunger? There is no caloric cost to that experiment. I have been advised by my dietician, and I have read in several books, to drink 8 to 16 ounces of water first thing in the morning before your feet hit the floor. Break the fast first thing in the morning with eight to 16 ounces of water. Have that water on your nightstand as hydrating first thing in the morning breaks the fast we endure while we sleep. This does three things, lubricates your spine, activates your digestive system, and

---

1   Benjamin Katz, Kayla Airaghi, Brenda Davy. Does Hydration Status Influence Executive Function? A Systematic Review, *J Acad Nutrition and Dietetics*, Volume 121, Issue 7, 2021, Pages 1284-1305 https://doi.org/10.1016/j.jand.2020.12.021.
(https://www.sciencedirect.com/science/article/pii/S2212267220315744)

2   Ganio MS, Armstrong LE, Casa DJ, McDermott BP, Lee EC, Yamamoto LM, Marzano S, Lopez RM, Jimenez L, Le Bellego L, Chevillotte E, Lieberman HR. Mild dehydration impairs cognitive performance and mood of men. *Br J Nutr*. 2011 Nov;106(10):1535-43. doi: 10.1017/S0007114511002005. Epub 2011 Jun 7. PMID: 21736786.

awakens your mind. In awakening the mind, you are enhancing the cortisol awakening response (CAR), which does more for your energy and alertness than coffee.

- *Cortisol*

Our third hormone, cortisol, is a stress hormone, giving a quick burst of energy and reduced sense of pain. Tapping into cortisol will enhance your ability to lead from the moment you get up. Your brain naturally releases cortisol throughout the day, including at night. In fact, the largest release is programmed to occur 30-60 minutes after awakening to kick-start your day. Break the fast with 8-16 ounces of water and put cortisol to work for you. If drinking water immediately upon awakening is the only thing you take away from this discussion, and you practice this every morning, you will feel the benefits immediately.

As the day progresses, refill your water bottle frequently. This seemingly mundane task carries with it other benefits. Walking through your building allows you to take the pulse of your corporate culture, catch people doing great things, and demonstrate your commitment to personal vitality and purpose to your team. Being visible, accessible, and personable with water bottle in hand are important contributors to your leadership style.

What if you know that drinking plain water is a non-starter, or have sensitive teeth that make pounding a ton of cold water unpleasant? There are many cheats. Vitamin C powders can make it easier to get that first glass down in the morning. Sugar-free water enhancements contain vitamins and flavors that can be squeezed into your water bottle. Eventually you could dial back the amount of flavors you need and acclimate to a mostly-water hydration regimen. There's nothing wrong with switching things up—the idea is to get yourself hydrated on a regular schedule throughout the day, beginning with 8-16 ounces first thing…before coffee or tea. You will feel the effects of your morning water immediately, day after day. Within a few days it will be a good habit, one that you can share with those you lead. Vegetables, fruits, yogurts (low fat or fat free) and soups all contribute to hydration as they all have a very high water content. Daily consumption of foods such as apples, oranges, watermelons, grapefruit, pineapples, cucumbers, carrots, celery, lettuce, strawberries, cauliflower and broccoli will energize you while keeping you hydrated. (Such foods are over 90% water.)

Enable hydration for those you lead by talking about it. Give everyone a water bottle with your company logo. Install water fountains with an automatic water bottle filler (like the ones we see in airport terminals, gyms, and hockey rinks).

DRILL:

1. Do the math to determine your required daily fluid intake. Bodyweight in pounds/2=number of ounces to be consumed daily. Body weight (lbs): _____ x 2 = _____ ounces daily

2. Obtain a metered fluid container (32-ounce Nalgene at home and at work makes it easier) and meter your daily intake, even if you don't hit the mark, you will at least be much closer through metering. Ounces of water daily: _____ ÷ 32 = _____ bottles

CHAPTER 9: NUTRITION

BLUF: 70% of chronic disease in America is preventable through diet

Factor number three is nutrition. "The life expectancy ranking of the United States among developed countries is likely to go into free fall, plunging from an already pretty dismal 43rd in 2016 to 64th in 2040."[3]

What is nutrition? Nutrition is the study of foods and substances in foods that allow for health and growth. How is it that one of the most developed nations in the world ranks 43rd in life expectancy? The average life expectancy in the United States is 79 years. A 2019 Forbes article indicates that cardiovascular disease is the leading cause of death for both men and women in the United States. Currently, cardiovascular disease is the costliest disease in our nation, with a price tag of $555 billion in 2016. Strategies that address major cardiovascular disease risk factors, such as high blood pressure and high cholesterol can significantly reduce the burden of cardiovascular disease to employers.

Another way to state the **BLUF** is that 70% of chronic disease in America is caused by poor dietary choices, and easily preventable. Yours truly is guilty. My cholesterol has been ticking up and up, and up, over the years. A few years ago I finally decided to do something about it, not through medication, but through diet, and the results were remarkable. My cholesterol came down almost 70 points in 30 days simply through dietary choices. But what does this have to do with leadership? Simple… the right food fuels the body and the brain and you need both physical energy and mental clarity to be the most effective leader you can be for the entire day, each and every day.

If you have the means, I recommend that you work with a dietitian and put yourself on a 30-day plan. Do some lab work and allow your

---

[3] Ref: https://www.healthsystemtracker.org/chart-collection/u-s-life-expectancy-compare-countries/

dietitian to create meals or meal plans for you that will help you achieve your physical objectives. Your objectives could vary from lose weight to gain weight, run faster, lift more, increase or decrease glucose levels, reduce resting heart rate, or become more physically flexible. When you learn what to eat, when to eat, and how to eat, you will find that you are energized throughout the day. More importantly, you will have mental clarity. In tough situations requiring snap decisions, you have this 360-degree awareness of what's going on allowing you to make the best decision possible.

On average, Americans working full-time spend more than one-third of their day, five days per week at work. When an individual goes all day without consuming nutrient-dense foods, their mental and physical health suffer, which can cause them to perform poorly. The workplace in general can be a roadblock to intentional, healthy eating. Workday meals in particular, especially breakfast and lunch, should be something that energizes you for the rest of the day rather than put you into what Daniel Pink calls a "trough," as discussed in chapter four. A trough is a time when you have difficulty focusing, concentrating, and getting things done. How can we put this into action? Simple. Prepare your meals ahead of time, especially lunch. While food preparation (food prepping) takes time, you will quickly discover that it is worth the effort. I was able to take the recipes from my dietician and prepared many of the meals myself. Alternatively, there are many businesses that will prepare your meals for you and then deliver them. In Virginia Beach I used Boxed Gourmet. They prepared meals based on the recipes and recommendations from my dietician. They deliver five days of meals every Sunday. For generally healthy meals that are not specific to my dietician, I use Clean Eatz, and there are several others. The cost ranges from roughly $6-$12 per meal depending on the type and quantity of protein. If you go out for lunch 2-3 times per week, you will be very happy with the savings and the result of eating healthy and energetic meals.

If you are bringing food from home, prep your lunch kit from leftovers the night before. Have your meals prepared, ready to go in the morning. Make sure they're nutritious and energizing meals. You'll reduce HALT-induced poor decision-making knowing that when lunchtime comes, all you must do is walk to the break room, grab that nutritious and energizing meal out of the refrigerator, go outside on a sunny day and enjoy your meal and get right back to work fully energized, ready to plow through the rest of the day. Healthy employees are happier, calmer, more engaged, sleep better and get sick less often. Just as with exercise in the next chapter, my measure for successful nutrition is my energy level and mental clarity throughout the day.

Many executives and others are tight on time and have to eat on the run, especially when they are traveling. It is still possible to eat well while traveling, and in many cases it is easier to find healthy options now than it was in the past. Grab-and-go salads, wraps, bottled smoothies, vitamin water, and fruits are all widely available. Fast food restaurants also serve high-protein, low-fat options but you have to work to find the best selection and then stick to it. If you are like me, do your research before you travel and become a creature of habit. Dial in on your hotel, look around on Google Maps to see what stores or restaurants are nearby, and make a plan to stock up your room refrigerator. This will save you time, keep you from being tempted by bacon and eggs, biscuits and gravy at the breakfast bar, and boost your productivity by giving you a few minutes to tackle email in your room. Ordering in also helps manage dinner "accidents" like the bloomin onion at Outback Steakhouse, or a dessert indulgence. (To be fair, eggs and biscuits are not bad, necessarily. We just need to watch portions and stick with higher-protein, lower-fat sides.)

There are times when group dining cannot be avoided. The continental breakfast doesn't have to be a disaster: yogurt, a banana and coffee is a great start to your day. The probiotics in yogurt are excellent for maintaining a diverse gut microbiota (collection of microbes living in your intestinal tract). In fact, this is a whole rabbit-hole we could spend 5000 words on. I won't do that to you (but my editor would love to!). I will add that intermittent fasting has shown great results overall. Many studies on intermittent fasting indicate that it improves, rest, overall nutrition, exercise, and brain and heart health. I am 45 days into intermittent fasting and I feel even more energized and alert. I am also sleeping better as my digestive system does not have to work while I am sleeping since I stop eating and drinking (other than decaffeinated tea or water) two-to-three hours before I fall asleep.

If you are trying to lose weight, tying in good nutrition with exercise, which we cover in the next chapter, will catapult your gains in executive function, greatly enhancing your ability to lead.

- *Serotonin*

I mentioned melatonin and HGH as they relate to rest, and cortisol as it relates to awakening. The fourth hormone that is key to your ability to lead is serotonin. Serotonin plays an important role in such body functions as mood, sleep, digestion, nausea, wound healing, bone health, blood clotting and sexual desire. Serotonin is a neurotransmitter that mediates satisfaction, happiness and optimism. Foods that can increase serotonin levels include eggs, cheese, turkey, nuts, salmon, tofu, and pineapple. If your breakfast and lunch contain the good stuff mentioned above, and little to none of the bad stuff, your serotonin levels will be higher, your executive function will be higher, your energy will be higher, your mood will be positive and energetic, and your ability to lead yourself and your team will be optimal.

Now that I have addressed the four hormones most under your control, you can hear a more detailed discussion in my podcast with Jerry Frentsos. Jerry is an author, educator, clinician, coach, and record-setting athlete in swimming. He describes his relay race between these four hormones and has written a great book on these topics: titled *Intentionally Well*.

Many mid-sized to large organizations have implemented workplace nutrition programs that encourage healthy eating among all employees, emphasizing fruits and vegetables and whole grain products; low fat dairy products, lean meats, poultry, fish, and legumes; and small amounts of salt, sugar, and saturated fat. These programs are often a component of a broader workplace health strategy that includes access to exercise instruction and equipment, which I address in the next chapter. How can you encourage your employees to eat healthy foods? You can keep the break room stocked with healthy snacks such as fruits, prepared vegetables, nuts, berries, and yogurt. Drinks can include electrolyte infused water and coconut water, as well as carbonated water. Mini meals such as packaged tuna or chicken, soups, and oatmeal are quick and easy to prepare. Within my organization I am fortunate to have a great teammate who is very health- and cost-conscious. She established a small commissary in our break room that has everything I mentioned above as well as many other items. She established an honor system for everyone on our team to have access to, and pay for, a variety of healthy snacks along with some not so healthy (but low cost) options. In the Navy we call this self-serve commissary a GeeDunk, or a coffee mess. In my experience most organizations have someone with this level of motivation, willing to put a GeeDunk together. You can seek out a volunteer as well. The importance of the position and the benefit this person brings to the team is more than noteworthy, and demonstrates leadership.

Another approach, if you have the means, is an intervention of sorts. Offer live health coaches to support your employees' physical and mental health delivered via a mobile app. Programs like RestoreHealth are used by Fortune 100 companies provide an up-front health risk assessment. A customized plan is then developed utilizing scientifically backed lessons, content, and curriculum that is paced based on each individual's needs. These programs focus on lifestyle behavior change around the four pillars of nutrition, exercise, stress management and sleep. Health coaches prompt individuals to acquire the skills, motivation, and support they need to alter their eating, food preparation, exercise, stress management, and sleep habits. Health risk appraisals and employee health surveys are continually used in combination with individualized clinical assessment, counseling on nutrition, and follow-up for the ultimate goal of sustained, healthy behavior change. Many health providers such as RestoreHealth work with individuals to develop detailed plans focused on a health-conscious lifestyle at work and at home. This investment in the wellbeing of your teammates contributes directly to the culture and values of your organization as discussed in chapter one. Not only do programs like RestoreHealth provide immediate return on investment via reduced medical claims spending, but they are valuable tools for employee recruitment, retention, productivity, and job satisfaction.

The final takeaway on nutrition is that having meals ready to heat and eat, especially at lunchtime, greatly reduces stress, saves time, saves money, nourishes the body, fuels the brain, and allows you to be highly energized and alert. I am not recommending a "diet" like the trendy diet plans we often hear of. I am recommending that you take control of your diet and make healthy choices as frequently as possible.

DRILL:
- Meet with a dietician or do your own research and develop a high energy diet.
- Conduct a 30-day experiment and record results daily. Results can include weight gain or loss, energy levels throughout the day, mental clarity, quality and quantity of sleep. You can also rate your perceived executive function.
- Seek input from your teammates regarding better nutrition in the workplace and implement one or two of the best recommendations.

CHAPTER 10: EXERCISE

BLUF: Make fitness a key component of your company culture.

Factor number four: Exercise.

This is where things really start to happen. Throughout my 26-year Navy Special Operations career, we conducted physical training (PT) on a daily basis, usually in the morning. This is just part of the military mindset, particularly in special operations. Regular PT strengthens the mind, body, and soul, while building relationships within the unit. PT helps set common expectations and creates readiness for any mission while bringing energy that lasts throughout the day. Some team members are great runners, others are better at pull-ups or push-ups, and some are average swimmers, like me. Working out as a team is a great way to appreciate different sets of skills within the team on any given day.

While these experiences are not easy to replicate in a private sector business, a shared passion for health and vitality is something that provides opportunity for everyday conversation (as you go fill your water bottle!). You might swap insights on training plans for an upcoming race, find a training buddy for your first 5k, or register as a group for a fundraiser walk/jog. The possibilities are endless and can include service as a part of your fitness initiative. A culture of fitness will boost overall company culture more than anything else because it says to each individual: your health is valued. Beyond these group dynamics, though, are countless other benefits that you reap personally. Your physical and mental wellbeing can be shaped by exercise in ways that the most potent drugs on earth cannot rival.

According to a 2019 Forbes article, statistics gathered by the U.S. Department of Health and Human Services show that only one in three adults achieve the recommended amount of physical activity each week, and more than 80% of adults do not meet the guidelines for both aerobic and muscle-strengthening activities.

Although I exercised regularly when I was active duty, I was not conscious that my brain and my body (my heart in particular) were actively messaging across signaling pathways. Sometimes I understood the messages, and sometimes I did not. Quite simply, when you elevate your heart rate to between 60% and 85% of your age-recommended maximum, a process called neuroplasticity is activated in your brain. These effects are concentrated in a particular area of interest to us. You guessed it: the prefrontal cortex[4], where executive function resides.

Neuroplasticity, the capacity of brain cells to change in response to internal and external factors, can have a negative or positive influence at any age across the entire lifespan. Neuroplasticity is the brain's ability to grow, change, adapt, and heal, among other things. Adherence to a healthy lifestyle has also been associated with enhancing vigorous longevity, health, happiness, and wellness. However, the opposite can also be true. In a 2016 study by Willey et al., a lack of leisure time physical activity was associated with cognitive decline.[5] We also know that aging is related to impaired cognition, but exercise can help prevent or reverse these effects. I read a book titled *Unstuck, Your Guide to the Seven-Stage Journey Out of Depression*. Although I am not, and never have been clinically depressed, this book was recommended by the great team at Marcus because of its prescriptions for good health and wellness. While it was written for the clinically depressed, the guidance in this book applies to anyone who wants to be on top of their game. Among the many recommendations to lift oneself out of depression, is exercise.

Some of my greatest moments of clarity have come either during or immediately after exercise. Many of my friends have verified this same sense of awareness and mental clarity either during, or immediately after moderate to rigorous exercise. One of my friends said that he wanted to put a white board in his shower because the shower makes him think of great things. I asked him what he was doing just before

---

[4] Basso JC, Suzuki WA. The Effects of Acute Exercise on Mood, Cognition, Neurophysiology, and Neurochemical Pathways: A Review. *Brain Plast*. 2017 Mar 28;2(2):127-152. doi: 10.3233/BPL-160040. PMID: 29765853; PMCID: PMC5928534.

[5] Willey JZ, Gardener H, Caunca MR, et al. Leisure-time physical activity associates with cognitive decline: The Northern Manhattan Study. *Neurology*. 2016 May 17;86(20):1897-903. doi: 10.1212/WNL.0000000000002582. Epub 2016 Mar 23. PMID: 27009261; PMCID: PMC4873686.

the shower and he said that he was at the gym. And quite simply, that's because we activated the cascade of hormones, growth factors and neurotransmitters which are responsible for feeding and repairing the brain. Lactate is produced by exercise, can cross the blood-brain barrier, is made independently *in* the brain, and is an alternate energy source for the brain (usually glucose is the go-to energy). A 15-minute exercise regimen was found to transiently increase lactate in the brain by about 20%.

Do you remember the hormone *cortisol* from the awakening response? Exercise also triggers the release of cortisol which affects mood, memory, and stress. The participants in a study who had the highest cortisol boost after exercise were the least affected by an experimental stressor.

I promised four hormones, but I'm adding a bonus fifth here. It is impossible to avoid mentioning dopamine.

- *Dopamine*

A mountain of studies demonstrate the positive effects on mood associated with exercise—you have surely heard about "runner's high." Initially thought to be dopamine-related, new research suggests that endogenous (made by the body) cannabinoids and opioids may be implicated to an even greater degree. Dopamine is secreted by anything that presents a challenge: leveling up on a video game, learning something new, successfully negotiating a deal, exercise, you get the picture. This is why edu-gaming has been so widely employed to help kids build reading and math skills.

Given these physiological benefits of exercise, you might consider getting a workout in before your most important cognitive demands of the day, such as an important meeting or presentation. You might also want to defuse stress before a challenging personnel meeting. More on this as we discuss brain and heart health in the next chapter.

Now when it comes to exercise I'm not talking about being a marathon runner, or a bodybuilder, or a world record-holder in swimming. I'm talking about taking note of how you feel on a daily basis. Are you energized? Do you have mental clarity? Does your energy and mental clarity last throughout the whole day? Do you look at your watch at five o'clock and think, "wow, where did the day go" because you were so energized throughout the whole day? The only way that happens is through rest, hydration, nutrition, and now exercise.

It's not even about what the scale indicates. It's about your energy level and mental clarity throughout the day, and without exercise your energy levels are going to deplete earlier in the day and your ability to be productive throughout the day, and your lifetime is going to be reduced. I will add that I am 56 years old as of this writing, and blood work/lab results are more important to me than how much I can bench press. In my twenties and thirties, running fast and lifting heavy weights was my measure of fitness. In my forties, avoiding, and recovering from, injury was my measure. Now, in my fifties, I care more about my lab results than how fast I can bike or how big my biceps are (well, I do try to maintain well developed biceps). As I mentioned in the previous chapter, my cholesterol tends to be elevated. But more than just cholesterol, there are many other blood factors worthy of your attention. Glucose, creatine, and testosterone (for men) can easily be increased or decreased through diet and exercise.

As a leader, everybody's watching you right down to what kind of shoes you're wearing. Set the example. Talk about exercise on a regular basis, provide fitness center passes or some way for your team to exercise, either at work, before work, during the workday (on the clock), or after work. Provide a healthy lunch for the crew from time to time. Workplace health and wellness programs are becoming the norm and are more important than ever. What exactly is workplace health and wellness and how can it benefit your company? An article in the December 2010 issue of the *Harvard Business Review* defines workplace wellness as an organized program that a company initiates for their employees and sometimes their employees' family members to help reduce health risks, to enhance personal effectiveness, to improve quality of life and to benefit the organization's bottom line. Organized workplace health and wellness programs are known to reduce overall healthcare costs for the employer and employee. Studies at the University of Michigan show that when employees stop smoking, lose substantial weight, and reduce cholesterol, employers can save roughly $2,500 per year per capita. A more healthy team member is less likely to miss work. Fit teammates experience less stress, and generally handle stress better, directly benefitting ROI. Companies with active and engaging health and wellness programs will experience less turnover, and perhaps attract better applicants. Employee loyalty to the company and commitment to teammates is greatly enhanced.

Set goals for yourself and discuss goals with others regularly, including during performance reviews. A fit workforce is a much more productive workforce, as proven by every branch of the US military. I have learned through experience that a fit workforce will be more focused on the task and less distracted by things that take away from solid productivity. From 5K runs to half matathons, I paid the registration fees for my teammates. On one occasion, I sponsored about 10 iFLY VA Beach staff in a memorial run for one of our EOD brothers who made the ultimate sacrifice. The draft beer at the finish line also makes for a great company event.

I started doing yoga about three years ago and that's been life-changing for me. Do you remember the serotonin discussion? Yoga, and meditation, enhance serotonin production. In addition to helping with my lower back pain, early morning yoga brings calmness and clarity that lasts the entire day. Big shout out here to my local yoga studio, Bliss Yoga, in Virginia Beach. Yoga encompasses not only exercise, it also includes breathing techniques that benefit brain and heart health. Most yoga studios now include corporate rates and memberships. Besides increased flexibility, I have less joint pain (almost none) and I can bend at the waist and knees in a way that I could not for the ten preceding years. I wish I would have taken up yoga 30 years ago.

A modern, state-of-the-art gym is not required. I've installed some basic fitness equipment within my business. I have a three-story facility and 40 people on my team. There is a fitness device called TRX. It is inexpensive, easy to install anywhere, and a great way to keep your team motivated about fitness. I have the TRX Suspension Trainer near the staff lounge, in my building. This simple, yet highly effective, suspension training system uses your body weight as resistance to help you work every muscle group and you can get a good cardio workout with TRX as well. The TRX is affordable, and via the app, includes 500+ workouts and programs for strength, cardio, yoga, and more with fresh content added daily, and makes a great gift (I am not paid by TRX for this endorsement, but maybe one day). It is amazing to see any of my 40 teammates use the TRX and other equipment that we have. I have seen the evolution of a new teammate go from not being too interested in using our modest workout station to working on getting that first pullup solo, or counting and supporting others, to mini group workouts lasting 3-5 minutes or so. I want to enable a culture of fitness. Remember, employee happiness comes from culture and values. Fitness, and access to a variety of fitness activities, contributes greatly to culture and values. There are now many corporate memberships that include thousands of gyms across the US and beyond. I even purchased a roller rink membership for one of my teammates (setting a benefit cap which is customizable to your employee's interests is one way to ensure equity without a one-size-fits-all approach). Health insurance companies are offering discounted premiums for good health habits that can be verified such as with lab work and regular health assessments with your primary care provider.

Commit to a lifestyle of fitness for yourself, enable fitness for those you lead, and make fitness a key component of your company culture. A culture of fitness will help you attract and retain the folks you want on your team.

DRILL: Determine your maximum heart rate, and 60% and 85% of your maximum heart rate. Then hit that zone for 30 minutes, 5 days or more per week through yoga, running/walking, biking, swimming, core or other cardio work, resistance weight routines…anything.

Maximum Heart Rate =

220 – (your current age: _____) = _____

60% of your maximum heart rate = _____

85% of your maximum heart rate = _____

Ask those you lead to determine their heart rate per above

CHAPTER 11: BRAIN-HEART LINK

BLUF: Slow is Smooth, Smooth is Fast

Your brain has a direct pathway to your heart through the autonomic nervous system. Your ability to influence others begins with the internal dialogue between your brain and your heart.

Think about your various promotions. Why were you selected preferentially? Were you able to see opportunities that others missed? Were you able to innovate solutions in the midst of chaos? Calmness of mind brings peripheral awareness. Leaders often must make decisions that are important, and possibly urgent. Each day we make decisions in our professional and personal lives. Often, we don't have all of the necessary information to make a decision, but good leaders will measure the risk and move out. Indecisive leaders hold up their team and ultimately lose confidence. Emotionally influenced decisions often have negative consequences. Emotional balance and mental clarity lead to better decision making. A strong connection between your brain and your heart will allow your internal emotional and mental process to slow, which increases reaction time. As we say in Special Operations, "slow is smooth, smooth is fast."

Thus, we arrive at <u>factor number five</u>: the brain-heart link. Let's just recap where we are. We previously reviewed the importance of sleep to recharge the brain, hydration, nutrition, and exercise. With respect to the link between brain and heart health, and how that impacts your ability to lead, recall our discussion of neuroplasticity (in Chapter 10). Neuroplasticity is the ability of the brain to grow, change, adapt and heal. Exercise is a mild stressor, causing the release of nerve growth factor which helps repair and replace nerve cells, just as sleep does (Chapter 7). Elevating your heart rate to 60 to 85% of your age-recommended maximum will cause changes in your brain's ability to conduct business and convey messages. This is why schools have found that putting a zero-hour PE class right before exams or a difficult subject is a good idea. But it must be remembered that this is a bidirectional pathway: If you want a healthy heart, you need a healthy brain, and a healthy brain is required to maintain a healthy heart.

The autonomic nervous system

The autonomic nervous system is a control system that acts largely unconsciously and regulates bodily functions such as the heart rate, digestion, respiratory rate, pupil response, urination, and sexual arousal. Within the brain, the autonomic nervous system is regulated by the hypothalamus.

The autonomic nervous system has two main divisions:

The sympathetic nervous system (SNS) and the parasympathetic nervous system (PNS). These two systems regulate the "fight-or-flight" response and the "rest and digest" state, respectively. Many organs are controlled primarily by either the sympathetic or the parasympathetic division. Sometimes the two divisions have opposite effects on the same organ. For example, the sympathetic division increases blood pressure, and the parasympathetic division decreases it. Overall, the two systems work together to ensure that the body responds appropriately to different situations.

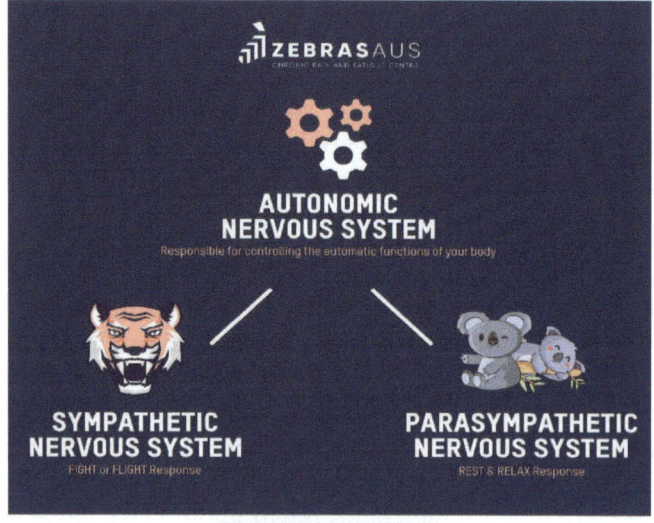

Fight, Flight, Freeze (and some include Fawn)

Let's begin with the SNS. When somebody cuts you off in traffic, your heart rate goes up, your blink rate goes up, your blood pressure goes up, peripheral vision literally narrows, and your ability to rationalize the situation is reduced. In short, you're angry (HALT). This also happens when the tiger is chasing you. This is called fight-flight-or-freeze. All you want to do is run from that tiger. That's your sympathetic nervous system taking you out of the driver's seat. This is when we are more likely to say or do things that we later regret. ("What was I thinking?")

Activation of the SNS can alter your typical composure and constrict your ability to weigh multiple pieces of conflicting information. For instance, somebody on your team could bring you very bad news (or even very good information!) and your SNS is going to want to take over. You may react impulsively, but this is not a good response for an executive. To prevent this from happening, you can activate your PNS to remain in control and respond in the best way possible.

Rest and Digest

We can control our SNS by engaging our PNS—the rest and digest mode. Leaders activate their PNS simply by breathing deeply. While there are several breathing techniques that are quite effective, simply making your inhalations shorter in duration than your exhalations, you will counter the activation of the SNS and activate the PNS.

For example, inhale for four to five seconds, pause, exhale for six to seven seconds. You can do this breathing technique a few minutes each day. Yoga classes often begin with a few minutes of breathing exercises. This is also a great technique to practice before a major event such as a very important meeting, or you can do this technique *during* an event, and you can certainly do it *after* an event to blow off steam. The point is to keep you in the driver's seat, keeping your comprehensive situational awareness at its peak. As I learned this information and began to deliberately activate my PNS, I felt much better about decision-making in general, and urgent decision-making in particular. You will learn to adapt to potentially dramatic situations by minimizing the drama. You are in control of yourself, plain and simple. Your display of calmness will bring calm and confidence to those under your charge. Let me repeat that… your display of calmness will bring calm and confidence to those under your charge. The opposite is also true. If you become agitated and frantic, your team will follow suit.

The next component of brain and heart health we will discuss as it applies to leadership is heart rate variability (HRV). As your body shifts from parasympathetic to sympathetic activation, your heart rate accelerates. You might have a linear, smooth heart rate acceleration, or you could have a very nonlinear, jagged heart rate acceleration. Shifting back to the parasympathetic state, your heart rate decelerates. With HRV, ideally these heart rate increases and decreases every second occur in a controlled manner....smooth gas, smooth brake. However, we often allow the sympathetic sytem to regulate...hard gas, hard brake. This is taxing on the heart-brain interface and drains your brain battery much faster.

As you might imagine, smooth acceleration is less taxing on the body or the mind. The jagged, irregular acceleration is mentally and physically exhausting. Have you ever had a day where you didn't really do anything physically demanding, but at some point in the day you asked yourself, "Why am I so mentally and physically tired?" It's probably because your autonomic nervous system transitioned between sympathetic and parasympathetic throughout the day, which your body naturally does anyway. But in this case, because of irregular heart rate variability, it was very exhausting.

Heart Rhythms Directly Affect Physical and Mental Performance

Heart signals affect the brain centers involved in emotional perception, decision making, reaction times, social awareness and the ability to self-regulate.

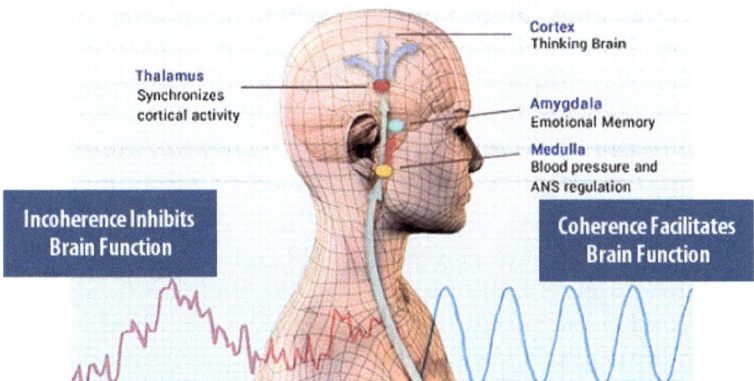

The graphic above from my HeartMath™ Skills workbook shows how our brain reacts to the signals from the heart. The red dot represents the amygdala, which is on guard, looking for signals from the heart. With poor HRV, the amygdala will send out emergency hormones such as cortisol and adrenaline, even when there is no tiger chasing you. This is mentally and physically exhausting. If we have good HRV, we maintain coherence, enabling higher brain functioning. If, due to lack of rest, hydration, proper nutrition, and exercise, we have poor HRV, we are in a state of incoherence, which reduces brain function.

How do we control our heart rate variability? You guessed it: rest, hydration, nutrition, exercise, proper attention to brain and heart health, and lifelong learning (which we will cover next in Chapter 12). Having smooth heart rate variability is like the calm *well before* the storm. It's the calm at the starting line—you're ready to go and your heart is ready to accelerate with you throughout the duration of the event. Ultimately, what good heart rate variability means is that you are calm, but highly aware, throughout the day, especially during a crisis. As you maintain and deepen your level of calm, you can think better and faster. This higher level of awareness allows you to see opportunities that others might not see. Or it allows you to create opportunities that might not otherwise exist, and gives you problem-solving tools that would not otherwise be available.

What does all of this brain and heart stuff have to do with leadership? Everything! You can prepare for an upcoming event that may be difficult, or you can recognize within yourself when the SNS is trying to take you out of the driver's seat and activate the PNS to remain calm, cool, and in 100-percent control. Practice a breathing technique prior to a presentation or important meeting. Even better is to regularly practice various breathing techniques through activities such as yoga and meditation. I highly recommend subscribing to HeartMath™ via a certified HeartMath™ coach. Monitor your heart rate and use deliberate techniques to keep you in a target heart rate zone appropriate for the situation. Regardless of what type of information your team brings to you, either very good news or very bad news, your response in both situations should be measured, calmly delivered, and accurate. This will build even greater trust among your teammates. If you are a leader with visible storm clouds over your head, people will not want to share information as readily, especially when it is bad news. In my experience, the sooner you get the bad news, the quicker you can ease the pain.

A final note on the brain-heart link: you may not realize that you are breathing with shallow breaths all the time when you are focused. Increasing the depth and length of each breath can help you clear your mind while you work, keep your blood pressure down, and oxygenate your mind. Try it.

In closing, let's go back to the concept of mono vs stereo sound. Mono is modeling the behavior you want to see from others on your team. Your team needs you to be calm, confident, and in control when things start to get difficult. Stereo is your ability to recognize the state of mind of your teammates, and that of the people you do business with. Through stereo awareness, you can mentor others to find a state of calm and handle the situation in the best manner possible.

DRILL:

1. Research three or four breathing techniques, practice them daily, then adapt to the one or two techniques that bring you calmness and awareness.
2. Find a blood pressure cuff and experiment with biofeedback. Your first reading will likely be high, the next lower. Record the diastolic and systolic readings.
3. Now try deliberately bringing down your blood pressure with biofeedback: breathe in and out slowly. Record the numbers over three readings.

CHAPTER 12: LIFELONG LEARNING

BLUF: Lifelong Learners become Lifelong Leaders

Factor number six, our final factor, is lifelong learning.

Education is not the learning of facts but the training of the mind to think- Albert Einstein.

Ok, Einstein violated my ground rule of avoiding absolutes, but, hey, it's Einstein. This is simple. If you've made it to Chapter 12, you're a lifelong learner, and being a lifelong learner is critical to lifelong leadership. The best leaders are constantly learning new things. Lifelong learning can be for both personal and professional reasons. On the personal side, you will enhance your social skills and your ability to participate in various organizations. On the professional side, you will significantly enhance your competitiveness when applying for a new job, increase your likelihood of promotion, and generally get better at what it is that you do. You can learn new things at home, at work, and while pursuing leisure activities. I also think it is good to have a mix of learning activities. By mix I mean that some activities can be self regulated or self paced, while other learning activities would include receiving instruction of some sort, like attending a class either in person or online.

Options for learning are infinite. You can read a book, pick up a guitar or ukulele and learn to play, attend college or university in person or online, develop trade skills such as carpentry or landscaping, reboot your foreign language skills by listening to podcasts in the target language, or find a language exchange partner using one of many apps—the opportunities are endless. Simply participate in almost any activity you can imagine, as long as it is new. When we learn new things, our brains create new neural pathways—the very essence of neuroplasticity discussed in the previous chapter.

As you get smarter your brain literally forms new synapses and becomes more capable. An example of this from neuroscience research[6] is a simple task: forming new memories, like where the car keys are. Those with mild cognitive impairment and healthy controls were randomized to a training activity to help them activate the hippocampus. The image below shows this region of the brain on a functional MRI (fMRI) scan. The people with mild cognitive impairment who received the training exercise showed more activity in the hippocampus than those in the control group, during both the storage and retrieval portion of the memory-building work.

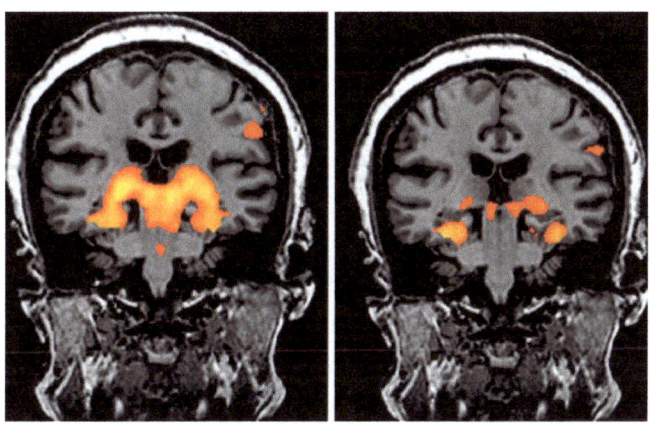

Courtesy Emory University. Source: https://news.emory.edu/stories/2012/02/memory_training_for_mci/index.html

In recent years I've pushed boundaries myself: I learned how to snowboard at the age of 49. As a skier since childhood I could have stayed in my comfort zone, but I decided to learn how to snowboard. It was not easy falling on the bunny slope in front of my twin teens, I guarantee you! But for the past five years I have been snowboarding with them and have enjoyed dramatic improvement. This also led to a family trip out West every winter. I also coach youth hockey and attend hockey coaching clinics every year, called continuing education

---

6   Hampstead BM, Stringer AY, Stilla RF, et al. Mnemonic strategy training partially restores hippocampal activity in patients with mild cognitive impairment. *Hippocampus* 2012;Feb. https://doi.org/10.1002/hipo.22006

programs (CEP) for hockey coaches, hosted by USA hockey. These programs not only teach me how to be a better hockey coach, they teach me how to be a better father, a better husband, a better leader in my business, a better member of the local community, and a better human being (and how to moderate drinking despite having a great time with fellow hockey players!). I also learned how to ballroom dance about three years ago. Never in my wildest dreams would I have previously thought about participating in a competitive ballroom dance, but I did it to raise money for a charity. The experience challenged me tremendously because—like anyone—I don't particularly enjoy being the newbie and looking foolish. Thankfully, I learned long ago that taking myself less seriously and being a good sport is a great way to forge team morale. Despite being far outside of my comfort zone, I had a great time learning and now guess what? I'm glad I have that skill. You just never know when it will come in handy... I learned a lot and I met some wonderful people. Even better, most of my employees got behind the effort and the event was great fun for all. I know that my team appreciates my efforts to be a leader in our community as well as in my business. I believe events like this dance experience bring additional pride to everyone on my team, further contributing to great culture. As they see their leader cha cha outside of his comfort zone, ideally, this will inspire them to further challenge themselves.

Writing this book has been, and continues to be, an incredible learning experience. In my podcast discussion with Brad McDonald, we talked about how the writing process is a learning experience. In my case, I learned much more about myself and the topics that I thought I was already well-versed in. The more I write with the intent of informing you, the reader, the more I inform myself. I have also developed a rhythm to my writing, and will continue to refine this process.

Other examples of lifelong learning include Warren Buffett reading for six hours a day. Mark Cuban reads for three hours a day. General James Mattis, a revered military leader and retired four-star general who wrote the book *Callsign Chaos*, states that "if you haven't read hundreds of books, you are functionally illiterate. You will be incompetent because your personal experiences alone aren't broad enough to sustain you." I will simply say this: such advice comes from a man who knows what he's talking about. It has been said that roughly 33 percent of U.S. high school graduates never read a book after high school and 50 percent of books started are never read to completion. I am guily of the latter. Sadly, 70% of adults have not been in a bookstore in the past five years.

I maintain a modest library of 50 books or so in the conference room of my facility and promote reading often. Topics on our bookshelf include personal and professional growth, and business acumen.

The various forms of learning are endless. Highly effective leaders share what they have learned with others. In discussing new concepts, ideas that will benefit your team and your company will often flow from others due to your inspiration. Here are a few more things you can easily put in place to enhance your lifelong learning: audiobooks, podcasts, coaching youth or adult sports, hiring a leadership or business coach (or better yet, training to become a certified leadership or business coach), and attending training events such as clinics and workshops. These opportunities are easy to find on social media. Regarding all things leadership, treat your brand of leadership like your favorite hobby…know as much as you can about the subject, and share this knowledge with others.

I got serious about golf a few years ago and have since learned the nuance (aka frustration) of the game. Although not yet a scratch golfer, I play bogie golf or better regularly. Like most experiences I've described thus far, there are unforeseen positive aspects of learning something new. In addition to meeting new people and reconnecting with friends of the past, I now golf regularly with a retired EOD teammate who is quite active in his pursuit of health and wellness. As we chase the golf ball around the course, Stephen and I discuss many things including our most recent experiences in the treatment of PTSD and TBI. We both are incredibly fortunate to have access to so many veterans' programs regarding health and wellness, and this leads to even more learning.

One learning opportunity that Stephen and I recently discussed while playing a round of eighteen holes is learning a foreign language. Most of us remember our high school experience—either enjoying language-learning immensely or not so much (my experience). However, this can be quite fun, depending on one's natural ability to adapt to sounds and the rhythm of speech. The Department of Defense uses the Defense Language Aptitude Battery (or DLAB) to measure one's aptitude to learn a foreign language. DLAB is designed to measure language-learning potential, not current knowledge. While one cannot study specific practice questions for the DLAB, one can study grammar and English textbooks to ensure they have a solid grasp of English grammar before taking the test. Elements of the test include the ability to recognize accentuation and stress patterns in words and knowing where syllable breaks are in words. Stephen took the DLAB and learned to speak Spanish at the Defense Language Institute, Foreign Language Center (DLIFLC), located in Monterey, California. DLIFLC provides culturally based foreign language education, training, evaluation, and degree programs for the Department of Defense. Learning the language and culture of ally and adversary is critical to afford a comprehensive understanding of the operational environment, helping establish the *ground truth* as discussed in chapter one. Learning a foreign language and culture gives a competitive edge to our warfighters, and to anyone seeking to do business nationally and internationally.

The Department of Defense classifies foreign languages into category I-IV languages based on the difficulty of language acquisition for native English speakers (I being the most proximal to English and IV being the most distant due to alphabet, sentence structure and other criteria). Category I includes Dutch, French, Italian, Portuguese, and Spanish. Category II includes German. Category III languages include Belorussian, Czech, Greek, Hebrew, Persian, Polish, Russian, Serbian/Croatian, Slovak, Tagalog, Thai, Turkish, Ukrainian, and Vietnamese. And for all you overachievers and go getters, category IV includes Arabic, Chinese, Japanese, and Korean.

Having lived in Italy for three years and having grandparents who immigrated from Italy, I had a natural interest in becoming conversational in Italian. I also like to eat. When living in Italy, it is much easier to enjoy a dining experience if you can converse with the staff. The same is true for every other country I have visited. The fun is amplified when you begin to *dream* in the language that you are learning—this signifies real progress assimilating those new neural connections! Given the many countries I visited throughout my military career, I found it quite useful to learn 100 or so words in the language of the country I was headed to. There are many great tools to learn a new language. Prior to the introduction of Rosetta Stone and Babbel, the best learning tool we had was conversing with someone who knew the language. This is also quite fun and an app called Tandem provides a safe platform to find a compatible partner for text-based or live conversation. Having spent 10 months in Thailand over a 3-year period, the 100 or so words that I used regularly made each visit fun, productive, and full of great dining experiences.

Professional certifications are another great way to increase your competence and confidence. From welding to coaching to piloting an airplane, the variety of opportunities is expanding daily, such as drone piloting, as are the modes of learning. Other mind-sharpening activities include puzzles, cards, and strategy games. Lumosity, the online brain exercise website, trains cognitive skills such as memory and attention. Wordle and Redactle are two addictive-in-a-good-way games which expand your vocabulary and fluency in a variety of topics. You can train yourself to solve a Rubik's Cube. When my son was 12 around years old, he was a master at solving the cube and taught me how to solve it. There are books and websites to teach you how to solve this and many other puzzles.

Certainly, all of these activities serve you as a leader in ways you may not anticipate. Learning stimulates brain function, picking up a new skill keeps you connected to others outside your immediate social network, coaching and mentoring expands your awareness of the forces which shape society and the needs of younger people. Together, all of these things help you adopt and maintain a wide angle view with high energy and social fluency. Recall our discussion about blind spots in Chapter 6—this expansive consciousness will help you seize opportunities quickly and flag blind spots in your thinking before they explode in your face.

In leading your organization, model the behavior of lifelong learning and enable it for those you lead. Provide time and tuition fees (within reason) for anyone on your team who wants to advance their knowledge, skills, and abilities. Once again, the learning opportunities are endless. Going back to our last Ground Rule, select a new learning experience and have fun.

DRILL:

- Develop a reading, audio book, and podcast list.
- Identify 2 things that you want to learn for each calendar year, and dedicate the time and resources to cross the finish line.
- Share what you have learned with others.
- Ask others to share what they have learned with you.

FM 3-05.211

GO

GO

6-14. The jumpmaster commands GO when the aircraft is over the release point and the green jump light is on (Figure 6-13).

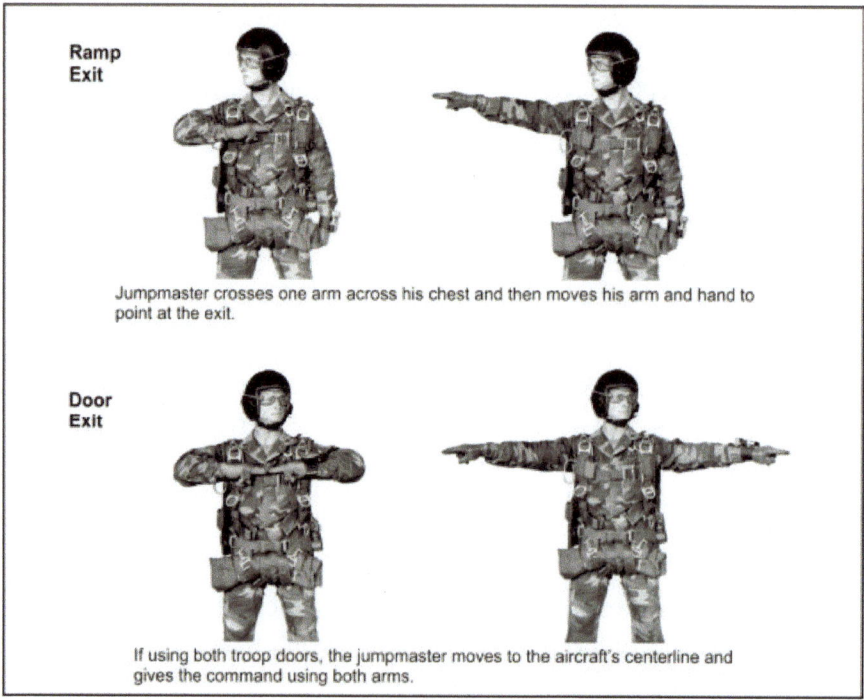

Figure 6-13. Go Command

"Go," is the final Jumpmaster command in military parachuting operations. One short, simple word, with so much riding on it. Upon receiving the "GO" command, each jumper is committing to execution that cannot be reversed: a true *fait accompli*.

The work that everyone on the team put in to get to "GO" is vast. Literally hundreds of hours and millions of military dollars were spent, with check points along the way. All of my teammates in the stick of jumpers relied on me to commit, just as I relied on them. We all relied on, and trusted, each other. Upon exiting, especially at night, each jumper is on his or her own during the freefall, parachute deployment, and canopy navigation to the LZ. Upon landing, the team regroups, determines azimuth, and moves to the target.

Take what you have learned in this book and *GO*.

Go build your personalized brand of leadership.

Go be the leader that your team needs.

Go be the leader that you would want to follow.

Go inspire everyone in your sphere.

Go build pride and confidence among those who rely on you—and those who don't.

Go give as much as you can, because the return on giving of yourself is the greatest reward of all.

Go Elevate Your Leadership.

NOTE TO READERS

Congratulations! At this point you should be energized and ready to lead your team through any situation.

Leadership is a perishable skill. It must be honed and practiced. For those of you already living the concepts I discussed, I hope your thoughts were validated—important concepts are worth revisiting often, confirming their significance. For those of you growing as a new leader, I hope this book helped you awaken to your potential to influence and inspire while keeping yourself healthy and fortified with the reserves you need to spot opportunities and deal with the chaos of uncertainty.

Now that we have constructed your foundation in leadership, my next book, *Elevate Your Team*, will give you the tools to build and lead a high-performing team. My experience in the military has taught me that we don't always get to pick our teammates, but we are expected to build the best unit regardless of our entering capacity. In the civilian world, leaders often have the opportunity to refine the team composition, but this takes time. Learning to lead the people you have is a vital skill.

Thank you for investing your time and money in *Elevate Your Leadership*. I would greatly appreciate a book review on any of the online platforms. Please visit RobertPizzini.com to learn more about my offerings, including my most recent articles and podcasts. And bring your team to iFLY Virginia Beach for an energetic approach to leadership development!

ABOUT THE AUTHOR

Robert (Bob) Pizzini is an accomplished leader and an active, award winning, CEO of his multimillion-dollar business. He was a US Navy Deep Sea Diver and Explosive Ordnance Disposal (EOD) technician for 26 years, leading missions to locate, render safe, and detonate explosives of all types, on land and under water, in some the most austere locations around the world. Bob coaches and mentors business and organizational leaders, high potential team members, political figures, academics, and others in the areas of personnel and professional development, business operations, organizational architecture, leadership, health and wellness as it relates to leadership, and building and leading high performing teams. He is active with the Hampton Roads Chamber of Commerce, various foundations, and coaches high school ice hockey.

Printed by Libri Plureos GmbH in Hamburg, Germany